ORI HELLERSTEIN

THE ARTISAN
BAKER

ORI HELLERSTEIN

THE ARTISAN
BAKER

with foreword by
MATTHEW FORT

Photography by Sue Atkinson

CONNECTIONS
BOOK PUBLISHING

For my beautiful wife and son, Yvonne and George.

A CONNECTIONS EDITION
This edition published in Great Britain in 2015 by
Connections Book Publishing Limited
St Chad's House, 148 King's Cross Road, London WC1X 9DH
www.connections-publishing.com

Text copyright © Ori Hellerstein 2015
Photographs copyright © Sue Atkinson 2015
This edition copyright © Eddison Sadd Editions 2015

British Library Cataloguing-in-Publication data available on request.

ISBN 978-1-85906-396-5

1 2 3 4 5 6 7 8 9 10

Phototypeset in Trajan Pro and Swiss 721 BT using InDesign on Apple Macintosh
Printed in China

CONTENTS

FOREWORD

by Matthew Fort

There I was in Stroud Farmers' Market in Gloucestershire, one of the finest in the country, wondering what to do about bread. There was one well-established bread stall, whose admirable products I had been munching for some years, but I was looking for something new, something different to tickle my jaded tastebuds.

Then I saw The Artisan Baker. The stall was a modest affair, tucked away in Swan Lane leading to The Shambles, but the bread looked anything but modest. You can tell whether bread has been made by a passionate baker just by looking at it. It has a kind of perky look to it, confident, all loved up. The crust is properly crusty. The colours have a certain burnish. The shape is plump and inviting.

Well, that's what I thought when I saw Ori Hellerstein's loaves for the first time, and standing behind them was Ori's wife Yvonne – one of those delightful people who sells those loaves with a smile that leaves you feeling cheerful even though you've just bought twice as much bread as you intended.

There was one bread in particular that attracted my attention. It was about 15cm (6in) long and about half that high at its tallest point, darkly bronzed and speckled with seeds. The top had a fissure running along it, as if it was bursting with good things. Which it was. It's called the Nelson Loaf and I've just had a couple of slices toasted for breakfast, and it tastes just as delightful as it did the first time I ate it.

The Nelson Loaf is named after Nelson Mandela, and stands proudly in the line of South African seed breads, which tells you something about Ori's approach to his craft. He's not a traditional baker in the sense of having been born and bred into it. Born in Israel, he trained at the Le Cordon Bleu Cookery School in London, and did time in various restaurants. But he wanted to make his own bread, in his own time, in his own way. And that leaves him free to produce his own, distinctive products, whether it be focaccia, sourdough or mince pies.

So he and Yvonne moved to Painswick, which was a sensible thing to do, and set up The Artisan Baker, which was an inspired thing to do – particularly for those of us who'll be popping by the stall next Saturday.

Now, if you're not in the happy position of being able to get there, then you can make your own versions of Ori's impeccable breads and other creations, thanks to the recipes in this book.

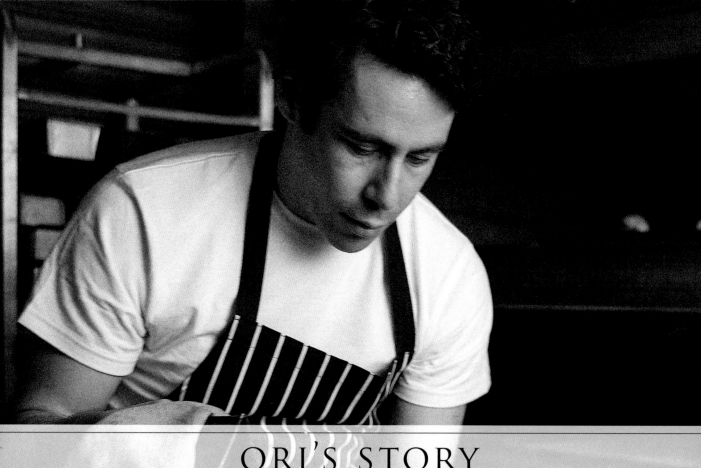

ORI'S STORY

I was born in Jerusalem, Israel, in 1981. My mother ran a delicatessen in the German Quarter of the city for most of my childhood, where I could often be found helping out – and drinking Coca-Cola and eating Twix bars (a real treat to have imported to Israel) after school! That was the beginning of what would turn out to be a lifelong passion for food.

After leaving school at the age of eighteen, I spent four years in the army as an officer, completing my compulsory military service. I then went to work as a waiter in a local restaurant, soon progressing to manager, and it was while taking a break travelling in Central America that I decided my passion would become my career. I moved to London to train at Le Cordon Bleu, where I studied classic French cuisine to superior level.

After graduating in 2007, I was delighted to get my first professional position as a demi chef in the pastry section at the Hilton Park Lane's award-winning Galvin At Windows restaurant. I then spent the next five years working in professional kitchens in London, eventually running my own pastry section.

In 2012, I moved to the Cotswolds with my wife Yvonne and our newborn son, taking the opportunity to act on my dream of setting up my own food business, The Artisan Baker. You can now find me baking in my Gloucestershire kitchen throughout the week and selling my range of artisan bread at Stroud Farmers' Market every Saturday, as well as running Costèllo + Hellerstein with Yvonne – our chocolate company making handcrafted luxury truffles.

For the last few years I have taught baking classes from my bakery in Stroud. The classes have been heavily oversubscribed, and I soon realized that there was a need for a simple baking book, to help home bakers achieve great results from their own kitchens. This is what inspired me to write THE ARTISAN BAKER. *I hope you enjoy making the recipes at home as much as I enjoyed creating them.*

Ori Hellerstein

INGREDIENTS

MAKING THE MOST OF LOCAL PRODUCE

Wherever possible, I try to use local produce in my baking. It's important to me to know where my ingredients come from, so I can trust that they have been grown and developed in a sustainable and healthy way; to support the local independent producers who fight for survival, day in, day out, with the large retailers; and to reduce the air miles of my food.

No matter where you are in the world, it's worth considering what is local to you and using it in the recipes. Here are a few examples:

• I tend to use GM-free extra virgin rapeseed oil instead of olive oil, as I live ten miles away from a rapeseed producer, but if you're local to an olive oil farm in Italy or Israel, then replace this with olive oil.

• Flour is easily changed according to where you are. Why not look into where your nearest flour producer is? I use Shipton Mill, as the flour is incredibly high quality and it's just down the road from our kitchens. When I first started the business, I'd drive to the mill in my old car and stack the boot full of 25kg bags of flour. Now we've grown, we get deliveries, but you'd be able to pop down to your flour mill, just the same!

• Consider changing the fruit in the recipes to something in season that you can find at your local greengrocer's, rather than something that's been flown halfway around the world.

You will find that the majority of the ingredients used in our recipes are easy to find at your local shops, but for the more specialist products I usually look online. For some of the more advanced recipes, you may need to plan ahead to ensure that you have all the ingredients, but it's worth it.

STORE CUPBOARD BASICS

BLACK TREACLE Also known as molasses, black treacle is a thick syrup and is a by-product of the processing of sugar cane or beet into sugar. (In some parts of the US, molasses also refers to sorghum syrup.) The quality of molasses depends on the maturity of the sugar cane or beet, the amount of sugar extracted and the method of extraction.

BROWN SUGAR comes either from the late stages of cane sugar refining, when sugar forms fine crystals with a significant molasses content, or from coating white refined sugar with a cane molasses syrup (blackstrap molasses). The colour and taste of brown sugar becomes stronger as the molasses content increases, as do its moisture-retaining properties. Brown sugars also tend to harden if exposed to the atmosphere, although proper handling can reverse this.

CAKE FLOUR is a finely milled white flour, made from soft wheat. It has a very low protein content – between 8 and 10 per cent – making it suitable for soft-textured cakes and cookies. The higher protein content of other flours would make the cakes tough. If you can't get hold of cake flour, use plain flour instead.

CASTER SUGAR This is the British term for a very fine sugar, so named because the grains are small enough to fit through a castor, a form of sieve. Commonly used in baking and mixed drinks, it is sold as 'superfine' sugar in the United States. Because it's so fine, it dissolves more quickly than regular white sugar and is therefore especially useful in meringues and cold liquids. Caster sugar can be prepared at home by grinding granulated sugar in a food processor for a couple of minutes.

CITRIC ACID is a weak organic acid. It is an antioxidant, a natural preservative and is used to add an acidic, or sour, taste to foods and soft drinks. Citric acid exists in a variety of fruits and vegetables, most notably citrus fruits. Lemons, limes and chokeberries have particularly high concentrations of the acid; it can comprise as much as 8 per cent of the dry weight of these fruits.

As a food additive, citric acid is used as a flavouring and preservative in foods and beverages, especially soft drinks. It is denoted by E number E330.

CONDENSED MILK Also known as sweetened condensed milk, this is cow's milk from which water has been removed and to which sugar has been added, yielding a very thick, sweet product that can last for years in the cupboard if unopened.

EXTRA VIRGIN RAPESEED OIL (NON GM) Rapeseed is the third most important crop grown in the UK, after wheat and barley; rapeseed and linseed are the only oils produced and bottled in the UK. Rapeseed oil comes from the black seeds of the rapeseed plant, *Brassica napus*, from the same Brassica family as the health-enhancing vegetables broccoli, cabbage and cauliflower. The plant produces sunny yellow flowers around springtime, so look out for golden fields brightening our beautiful landscapes during these months.

In the past, rapeseed oil has been overshadowed by its better-known Mediterranean counterparts, olive oil and sunflower oil; however, celebrity chefs, foodies and nutritionists alike are now recognizing and celebrating its culinary and nutritional properties. A cold-pressed rapeseed oil is a healthy choice, with less saturated fat than all other cooking oils and fats; it's also high in the beneficial monounsaturated and polyunsaturated fats omega 3, 6 and 9.

FAST-ACTION DRIED YEAST was developed in the 1970s and is the easiest type of yeast to use. It's simply stirred into the dry ingredients before adding the liquid. The process used to dry the yeast is very gentle, so few yeast cells are killed and, when hydrated, it works more vigorously than fresh yeast. This means you only need to use half as much compared with fresh yeast, as you will see in the following recipes.

NOTE: Dried yeast usually comes in 7g (¼oz) sachets, so where the amount required is easily divided or multiplied by 7g, the weight is given in the recipes. Other amounts are given in teaspoons.

FILO PASTRY Phyllo, filo or fillo dough or pastry is made up of paper-thin sheets of raw, unleavened flour dough, and is used for making pastries in Turkish, Greek and Middle Eastern cookery. Filo dough is made with flour, water and a small amount of oil. It is almost always used in multiple layers separated by melted butter. When these are baked, they become crispy and the result resembles puff pastry, though the method is very different; they are not generally substituted for one another.

Homemade filo takes time and skill. Using a very big table and a long rolling pin, the dough is rolled and stretched into a single thin, very large sheet, which is continually dusted with flour; the surface tends to break apart. Once finished, the filo is floured, folded, then used as desired. Most filo is made with wheat flour and water, but some dessert recipes call for egg yolks in addition.

FRESH YEAST is firm, moist and creamy beige in colour. Sometimes called compressed yeast, it can usually be bought from supermarket bakeries, bakers and baking suppliers. If stored in an airtight container, fresh yeast will last for up to 2 weeks in the fridge or 3 months in the freezer. Do not use fresh yeast if it has a strong, unpleasant alcohol smell or has become slimy. To use fresh yeast, gently dissolve it in some of the warm liquid used in the recipe. Alternatively, you can finely rub it into the flour before adding the salt, although this takes more time.

GLUCOSE is made from maize starch. It is used as both a sweetener and a thickener, in products such as syrups and caramels. It usually comes in the form of a clear thick liquid and is sometimes called glucose syrup or corn syrup. It's best to handle it with wet hands.

GOLDEN SYRUP is a thick, amber-coloured form of inverted sugar syrup, made in the process of refining sugar-cane juice into sugar, or by treating a sugar solution with acid. It is used in a variety of baking recipes and desserts. Golden syrup has an appearance similar to honey, and is often used as a substitute for people who do not eat honey. It can also be used as a replacement for corn syrup.

ICING SUGAR (or powdered sugar) is produced by grinding sugar to a fine powder. The manufacturer may add a small amount of anticaking agent (cornstarch or tri-calcium phosphate) to prevent clumping.

PECTIN is produced commercially as a powder, white to light brown in colour. It's mainly extracted from citrus fruits and is used in food as a gelling agent, particularly in jams and jellies. It's also used in fillings, medicines and sweets, as a stabilizer in fruit juices and milk drinks, and as a source of dietary fibre.

POLENTA is made with ground yellow or white cornmeal (ground maize). It can be ground coarsely or finely, depending on the region and the texture desired. Polenta derives from earlier forms of gruel or grain mush (known as *pulmentum* or *puls* in Latin), commonly eaten in Roman times and later.

Polenta is very similar to corn grits, a common dish in the cuisine of the southern United States, with the difference that grits are usually made from coarsely ground kernels. When properly cooked, grits and polenta have similarly smooth textures, 'grit' referring to the texture of the dried corn before cooking. Another variation uses ground hominy (similar to masa harina), lye-treated corn kernels.

ROSE WATER is used to flavour food; it's a by-product of rose oil, which is used in perfume. Rose water has a very distinctive flavour and is used heavily in Asian and Middle Eastern cuisine, especially in sweets – rose water gives loukoumi (Turkish delight) and gulab jamun (a popular South Asian dessert) their distinctive flavours. In Iran, it's also added, in small quantities, to tea, ice cream, cookies and other sweets; in the Arab world and India, it's used to flavour milk and dairy-based dishes such as rice pudding. It is also a key ingredient in sweet lassi, a drink made from yogurt, sugar and various fruit juices, and is used to make jallab (a fruit syrup enjoyed in the Middle East). In Malaysia and Singapore, rose water is mixed with milk, sugar and pink food colouring to make a sweet drink called bandung. In Western Europe, rose water is sometimes used to flavour marzipan and a shell-shaped French cake called a madeleine, which you'll find with different flavours in this book.

RYE is a grass grown extensively as a grain, a cover crop and a forage crop. Rye grain is used for flour, rye bread, rye beer, crispbread, some whiskies, some vodkas and animal fodder. It can also be eaten whole, as boiled rye berries, or rolled, similar to rolled oats. Rye is a cereal grain and shouldn't be confused with ryegrass, which is used for lawns, pasture and hay for livestock.

SELF-RAISING FLOUR Self-raising (or self-rising) flour is white flour that is premixed with chemical leavening agents. Self-raising flour is typically composed of the following:
- 110g (4oz) flour
- 1 teaspoon baking powder
- a pinch of salt

SEMOLINA is the cracked endosperm of wheat which is produced during the commercial milling process and is subsequently ground into flour. However, although most of the semolina produced is milled into flour, a small percentage of the output is sold as a food item.

SPELT Spelt grain is a cereal that has been found by archaeologists in many prehistoric sites and was popular in Roman times. Like wheat, spelt contains gluten and therefore produces good bread, which people prize for its flavour and its natural richness of minerals.

STONEGROUND WHOLEMEAL FLOUR Whole grains are cereal grains that contain germ, endosperm and bran, in contrast to refined grains, which retain only the endosperm. The stone grinding process involves a miller grinding the grain between two stones. They mill the grain gently, keeping it cold so the nutrients aren't 'cooked away'.

STRONG WHITE FLOUR has a higher protein content than plain white flour, and, as its name suggests, plenty of 'muscle'. When it's made into a dough, the flour absorbs water and, with kneading, creates long elastic chains of gluten/gliadin proteins, forming a superstructure which produces bread with more volume and an open texture.

WILD GARLIC Also called ramsons, wild garlic is a wild relative of chives. The bulbs, flowers and leaves are all very tasty. The leaves can be used in salads, as a spice, boiled and eaten as a vegetable, or used instead of basil in a pesto.

Ramsons leaves are also used as fodder. Cows that have fed on ramsons produce milk that has a slightly garlicky flavour, and butter made from this milk was very popular in Switzerland in the nineteenth century.

WILD RICE is actually a semi-aquatic grass that has historically grown in lakes, tidal rivers and bays, in water between 60cm and 120cm (2–4 feet) deep. It is one of only two commonly eaten grains that are native to North America (the other is corn), and it originated in the Great Lakes, which are situated on the border between the US and Canada.

EQUIPMENT

I have put together a list of equipment to help you to make the recipes in this book quickly, easily and without stress. Don't panic if you haven't got a particular item and don't have a neighbour you can borrow from – it's fine to use an alternative. For example: use a different-shaped tin; use butter to grease a tray, rather than an oil spray; use a spoon instead of a scraper, and so on …

If you are looking to purchase equipment, your local kitchenware shop should have most things that you'll need; alternatively, you'll find everything easy to come by online.

BAKING PAPER
There are different types of baking paper; always go for a good-quality option, as the cheaper ones can stick to cakes and tins!

BAKING SHEET
Flat baking sheets are great for baking bread or any of the savoury pastries in the book. They are a good size and are easy to line with baking paper.

DIGITAL SCALES
enable you to measure accurately. If your scales don't have a setting for liquids, you can easily convert millilitres to grams in order to weigh them on the scales: 1ml = 1g.

DIGITAL THERMOMETER
This is very useful when it comes to more advanced baking and is used in the recipes for Violet Macarons, Millionaire Shortbread, Mandarin Pâte de Fruits and Mini Cinnamon Doughnuts. You would struggle to make any of these without one, as they require precise heat measurement.

DIGITAL TIMER
It is helpful to have a second timer, as well as the timer on your cooker, so that you can bake two things at once.

ELECTRIC MIXER
Free-standing mixers don't come cheap, but if you can afford it (and have the space) I highly recommend that you get one – KitchenAid and Kenwood are good brands to choose. It will come in handy for most of the recipes in this book, and will reduce the energy you use on kneading, mixing, and so on. To knead dough using a mixer, place all the ingredients in the bowl and knead on low speed, using the dough hook (this should come with the mixer as standard), for 7–10 minutes.

GREASEPROOF SPRAY
Most recipes in the book require you to grease your tin or tray. The easiest way to do this is to buy a spray. As well as being convenient, it gives you an even distribution of grease without using a lot.

ICE CUBES   It's a good idea to keep a supply of ice cubes in the freezer; when you put a loaf of bread in the oven, throw an ice cube into the oven after the bread, to create steam. This will result in a lovely crust and will also prevent the crust from forming too early, allowing the bread to bake to its full potential.

MEASURING SPOONS   Many of the ingredients used in this book are measured in teaspoons or tablespoons. I suggest getting a set of measuring spoons that come on a ring – you should be able to find them in your local kitchenware shop. For powders, simply scoop the ingredient into a heap, then flatten it with your finger (1 tsp = 5g and 1 tbsp = 15g).

PIPING BAGS   I use these all the time, to pipe ganache, cake batter, and so on. Once you start using them, you'll see how easily you can get your cake batter into the silicone moulds, without causing a mess in your kitchen. I buy disposable ones in a roll of a hundred. You can, of course, get reusable piping bags; however, you may find that you can't pipe batter containing berries or nuts, as the hole is too small.

PLASTIC BOWLS   I recommend that you have a good supply of plastic bowls in different sizes, as they are very useful for measuring ingredients. However, if you were only to buy one or two, I would go for large bowls; they're perfect for kneading and proving dough.

ROLLING PIN   I have a few of these in different sizes and materials. Go for the heavy-duty plastic ones: a long one (30–35cm/12–14in long) to roll out dough, and a shorter one (about 15cm/6in long) for smaller pastries and doughs.

SCRAPER   I consider this to be the most valuable piece of equipment in my bakery; it's so versatile, and a real time-saver. I use it for mixing dough, scraping flour from the work surface and scraping dough and cake batter from the mixing bowl. I recommend that you have a plastic one with one end curved and a metal one with a straight end to help you clean your work surface.

SILICONE MOULDS   I use my silicone moulds for cakes, bread rolls and other baked goods, such as the Nutella Brioche, for which I used a mini-muffin mould to give them their shape. Silicone moulds are available in many shapes and sizes. Flexipan silicone moulds don't require greasing; the cakes will just pop out. They are very expensive but will last you a long time. Other cheaper brands are available, but you may find that you need to grease them before use.

SPATULA   Essentially a scraper with a handle – worth having if you don't want to get your hands dirty! A spatula is useful for folding cake batter and scraping the mixture into the tin; it will do a really thorough job, minimizing waste and improving cleanliness.

TINS   You will need to have a selection of loaf tins for bread and cakes, a number of round cake tins and a deep baking tray for traybakes, such as brownies and blondies.

WHISK   A good-quality hand whisk is a must-have for mixing cake batter; I also like to use a whisk, instead of a spatula, to very gently fold in some of the wetter cake batters.

BASIC TECHNIQUES

In this section you will find advice on the general techniques every baker needs to be familiar with, along with some pointers on what to look for and how to get the best results.

PROFESSIONAL TIPS

• Weigh all your ingredients into separate containers before you start, so everything is ready to go. Get your oven ready, your trays ready and all the necessary tools together.

• Rule number one in the baking industry: make sure you follow the recipe to the gram, otherwise you'll have problems. If you add too much flour to a bread recipe, for instance, the texture will be wrong and will result in dry bread. I recommend using digital scales, as they are the most accurate (*see Equipment, pages 22–5*).

• When proving dough, temperature is key. Ideally, all the main dough ingredients (flour, water … but not the yeast, if using fresh yeast!) should be at room temperature. If baking in winter in a very cold kitchen, use warm water; conversely, if in a hot kitchen during the summer, use cold water. The dough should then take the same amount of time to prove at the end. It's worth getting a thermometer to check your room temperature – it should be between 18°C and 24°C (64–75°F).

• It's really important to grease or line the baking tin or tray, for the simple reason that you're dealing with sticky ingredients. For bread, grease your loaf tin or baking sheet using a greaseproof spray or brushing with oil or softened butter. For large cakes, you can again use a greaseproof spray, or brush with fat, then line with good-quality baking paper.

• If you have trouble removing your cakes from the silicone moulds once they've cooled completely, pop them in the freezer for 1 hour, until semi-frozen, and you should find that they'll come out easily. Leave them to thaw for 20–30 minutes, before serving.

• To make sure your individual cakes are all the same height and evenly baked, as well as piping an equal amount of batter into the moulds, place a silicone sheet on top of the tray.

MAKING DOUGH

If you're making dough by hand, I would recommend that you start by putting the ingredients into a large bowl and using a scraper to bring everything together until it forms a dough – this is the messy part. Next, place the dough on a flour-free work surface. Knead the dough by stretching and folding it back. This will work the gluten. Use your scraper if the dough sticks to the bench, but don't be tempted to add any flour. The faster you knead, the more easily the dough will come away from the work surface. After 7–10 minutes, you will see that the dough no longer sticks to the bench. It should be very elastic.

If you're using an electric mixer, just put all your ingredients in the bowl and mix with the dough hook for 7–10 minutes, at medium speed.

PROVING

Most recipes require two proving stages. For the first, prove the dough in a large bowl and, as a general rule, leave it until the dough has doubled in size.

The second stage is a bit more tricky, as it's hard to know when the dough is ready to go into the oven. It's a question of learning from experience. If you're using a loaf tin, it's fairly straightforward – prove the dough until it's 1–2cm (⅓–¾in) above the height of the tin. If the dough is a freestyle shape, prove until it has increased in size by 150 per cent.

Round shapes will need more time to prove than longer or flatter shapes.

MAKING CAKE BATTER

Always use a large bowl and, if you're making a cake by hand, fold the ingredients in using a large whisk. Don't mix vigorously; just fold the ingredients in very gently. Overworking the batter will result in a tough cake.

When creaming butter and sugar together, beat until they turn a very pale colour and have substantially increased in volume. I recommend using an electric mixer with a paddle attachment.

To combine eggs and sugar, beat together until pale and substantially increased in volume. Again, I recommend using an electric mixer for this, but with a whisk attachment. Beat at high speed, then reduce the speed to fold in the remaining ingredients.

Temperature is very important. Make sure all your ingredients are at room temperature, to avoid the mixture splitting. If the eggs are too cold, place them in a bowl and run hot water over the top. Cover and leave to stand for 3–4 minutes.

When adding eggs to a butter-based cake, drop them in one by one, each time adding a handful of the dry ingredients. Fold the mixture slowly.

Oil-based cakes are straightforward – you won't need to worry about the mixture splitting. Simply combine the sugar and oil, then add the eggs one by one, until you have a texture that resembles mayonnaise. Then fold in all the dry ingredients.

SHAPING BREAD ROLLS

Divide the dough into equal-sized pieces, weighing between 80g (2¾oz) and 100g (3½oz) each.

Use the middle of your palm to roll each piece of dough into a ball, curving your hand slightly, rotating your hand clockwise and pressing against the work surface. This technique takes a lot of practice to perfect. For me, the faster you rotate your hand, the easier it is to achieve the perfect roll shape.

SHAPING A TIN LOAF

Flatten the dough into a rectangular shape, then fold in 3–4cm (1¼–1½in) at each end. Fold the dough towards you in three stages, so that the ends meet (rather like an envelope).

Use the heel of your palm to ensure that the ends are firmly stuck together.

Place the dough in the loaf tin, smooth side up. Sprinkle flour over the top and leave to prove for the second time.

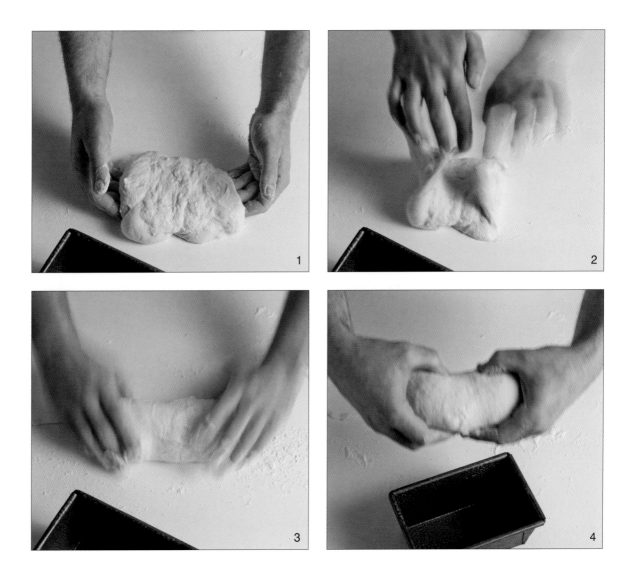

SHAPING COOKIE DOUGH

Place the cookie dough on a floured surface and divide into two halves. Roll each piece into a sausage shape, wrap in clingfilm and place in the freezer for at least 2 hours.

Cut off the clingfilm, place each cookie-dough sausage on a chopping board and cut into 1cm (⅓in) slices using a sharp knife.

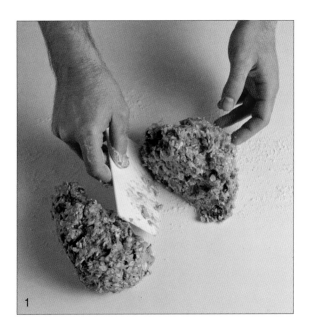

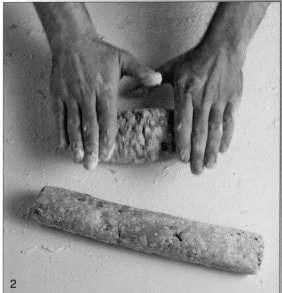

DIPPING COOKIE DOUGH

Have to hand a bowl of caster sugar and a bowl of icing sugar.

Divide the cookie dough into equal pieces and shape them into balls by rolling them between your palms. Dip the cookie balls first in the caster sugar, then in the icing sugar. Shake off the excess icing sugar, then place the balls on a baking sheet lined with baking paper. The sugar coating will give a crackled effect to the top of the cookies as they bake.

BREAD

OVERNIGHT WHITE

I like a white loaf, don't get me wrong, but I do always feel like I need another slice … and another slice … and another slice, to get any flavour. So, I wanted to create something strong in flavour, therefore allowing me to avoid overeating! We spent a good few weeks perfecting the yeast balance to ensure the dough didn't over-prove during this 17-hour process. It's now one of our most popular loaves.

330g (11½oz) strong white flour
210ml (7⅓fl oz) cold water
20g (⅔oz) yogurt
1½ tsp sea salt
1½ tsp caster sugar
7g (¼oz) fresh yeast or 3.5g (⅛oz) fast-action dried yeast

EQUIPMENT
1kg/2lb loaf tin

Place all the ingredients in a large bowl and combine to form a dough (*see Basic Techniques, page 28*). Transfer the dough to a floured surface and knead for 10 minutes, then place in a large bowl and cover. Leave in the fridge overnight.

NEXT DAY
Shape the dough and place in a loaf tin (*see Basic Techniques, page 32*). Leave to prove until the dough has risen above the top of the tin. This should take 1½–3 hours, depending on the temperature of the room.

Preheat the oven to 230°C/450°F/Gas 8 and bake for 30–35 minutes.

Remove from the oven and place on a cooling rack for 30 minutes before slicing.

Why not try …
replacing half of the white flour with wholemeal flour, if you like something a little browner.

WILD-RICE LOAF

35g (1¼oz) wild rice

50g (1¾oz) strong white flour

150g (5oz) wholemeal flour

60g (2oz) jumbo oats

40g (1½oz) black treacle

½ tsp sea salt

160ml (5½fl oz) water

30ml (1fl oz) sunflower oil

7g (¼oz) fresh yeast or 3.5g (⅛oz)
  fast-action yeast

EQUIPMENT

500g/1lb loaf tin

I first came across wild rice added to bread on the Caribbean island of St Lucia. It was a fantastic wholemeal loaf with wild rice sewn through it. I really enjoyed the texture and wanted to create my own version. It's simple to make, with only one proving stage. I love to eat it with cottage cheese and a simple salad – it doesn't need much more!

Pour the rice into a large pan and add plenty of hot water. Bring to the boil, reduce the temperature and leave to simmer for 40 minutes. Drain, then wash the rice in cold water.

Meanwhile, place all the other ingredients into a mixing bowl, except for 10g (⅓oz) of the oats, and mix with a dough scraper. Once it starts to form a dough, leave it in the bowl and use your hands to knead for about 10 minutes. The dough will be very wet, but that's OK – don't add more flour!

Add the wild rice to the dough and continue kneading until the rice is fully incorporated. Pour the dough into a greased loaf tin, brush the top with water and sprinkle on the remaining oats. Leave to prove for around 1–1½ hours, until increased in volume to approximately 1cm (⅓in) above the rim of the tin.

Preheat the oven to 190°C/375°F/Gas 5 and bake for 50 minutes.

Remove from the oven and place on wire rack to cool for at least 30 minutes before slicing.

Why not try ...
using sunflower seeds instead of the wild rice, for a different flavour and texture.

Stoneground Wholemeal

Wholemeal bread is a staple when it comes to bread eaten at home. It's fast becoming as popular as white, due to its healthier credentials, and, for me, it's a more interesting option than white, with a bigger flavour. We use a recipe with a 50:50 ratio of white flour to wholemeal, to avoid making the bread too heavy. I love to use stoneground wholemeal flour, as it retains the goodness of the whole grain within the flour. However, it's not essential and any wholemeal flour will work. This loaf should be perfect for sandwiches or toast.

Makes 1 large loaf or 7 80g (2¾oz) bread rolls

165g (5¾oz) strong white flour
165g (5¾oz) stoneground
  wholemeal flour
220ml (7½fl oz) cold water
20g (⅔oz) yogurt
1½ tsp sea salt
1½ tsp caster sugar
4g (½oz) fresh yeast or ½ tsp
  fast-action dried yeast

Place all the ingredients in a large bowl and bring together to form a dough (*see Basic Techniques, page 28*). Transfer to a floured work surface and knead for 10 minutes. Place the dough in a large bowl, cover and leave to prove at room temperature until doubled in size (this should take about 2 hours).

Meanwhile, line a baking tray with greaseproof paper.

Shape the bread dough into a loaf or divide and shape into rolls (*see page 31*), as desired, then place on the prepared tray. Leave to prove until increased in size by about 150 per cent (this should take 15–20 minutes for rolls and 30 minutes for a loaf).

Preheat the oven to 230°C/450°F/Gas 8. Bake for 30 minutes for a round loaf or 15–20 minutes for 80g (2¾oz) bread rolls.

Remove from the oven, transfer to a cooling rack and leave to cool for 30 minutes before serving.

Why not try …
adding 80g (2¾oz) of mixed seeds to the dough to create a granary loaf.

FOCACCIA

330g (11½oz) strong white flour
1 tsp sea salt
1 tsp caster sugar
12g (scant ½oz) fresh yeast or 6g (⅕oz)
  fast-action dried yeast
230ml (7¾fl oz) warm water
35ml (1¼fl oz) extra virgin rapeseed
  oil, plus extra for brushing and
  drizzling (or olive oil if you can't find
  rapeseed oil)
polenta (for sprinkling)
Maldon sea salt (for sprinkling)

I learned how to make focaccia when I was working in London; it's an absolute staple in any great restaurant. When I set up my own bakery, I tried to use as many local ingredients as possible and discovered that the local rapeseed oil produced in the Cotswolds was a great alternative to the imported Italian olive oil that's usually used in a focaccia recipe. The rapeseed oil gives the loaf the most incredible earthy flavour. This is my showstopper loaf at our local farmer's market stall – it's nearly a metre in length and half a metre wide; we slice it into huge pieces to eat on the street or take home.

Here's how to make your own smaller version.

Place the dry ingredients, yeast and water in a mixing bowl fitted with a dough hook. Knead the dough at low speed for 10 minutes and then add the rapeseed oil. Gradually increase the mixing speed until all the oil is incorporated into the dough. Alternatively, mix the ingredients together using a scraper, then knead the dough by hand for 10 minutes (*see Basic Techniques, page 28*). Add the oil and knead again until all the oil is absorbed.

Place the dough in a large bowl, cover and leave to prove at room temperature (18°C/64°F) until doubled in size (this should take about 1½ hours).

Remove the dough from the bowl, place it on a floured surface and roll into a smooth ball. Leave to rest for a few minutes.

Meanwhile, brush your baking tray with rapeseed oil and sprinkle with polenta.

Using your hands, flatten the dough a little and place it on the prepared tray. With the tips of your fingers, press the dough into an oval shape, about 2cm (¾in) thick. Brush the top with rapeseed oil, loosely cover with clingfilm and leave to prove again for 15–20 minutes.

Preheat the oven to 210°C/425°F/Gas 7.

When proved (risen by about 50 per cent this time), make holes all over the focaccia dough using your fingers, and sprinkle the top with Maldon sea salt. Bake for 20 minutes (baking time may vary depending on your oven), until the top is golden brown and the bottom is golden and slightly crisp.

Remove the focaccia from the oven, transfer to a wire rack and pour over lots of rapeseed oil and a good sprinkling of Maldon sea salt.

Why not try ...
adding 20g (⅔oz) of sun-dried tomatoes and 30g (1oz) of green olives to the dough after brushing with oil and before proving for the second time.

▶ *key stages illustrated overleaf*

FOCACCIA KEY STAGES

1. Combine the ingredients in a large bowl, using a scraper.

2. After kneading, add the rapeseed oil to the dough.

3. Knead again until the oil is absorbed.

4. Flatten the dough a little and place it on the prepared baking tray.

5. Use the tips of your fingers to press the dough into an oval shape.

100% RYE

*I'll never forget the first time I tasted 100% dark rye bread. When
I was a teenager I worked in my mother's deli in the centre of
Jerusalem. One day, a slightly strange-looking man with a strong
Russian accent walked into the shop and insisted we try a loaf
of bread that he pulled from his backpack. It was the darkest and
heaviest loaf I had ever tasted, but it was perfectly moist and
delicious. We ordered a dozen loaves on the spot and he became
one of my mum's favourite suppliers. I wanted to create a loaf
just like it when I set up my bakery.*

Slice thinly and eat with a light soft cheese and salami.

First, place all the ingredients for the sponge in a large bowl, mix well
and leave for an hour, or until the mixture has doubled in volume.

Next, put all the dough ingredients in a large mixing bowl, add the
sponge and mix well until combined.

Transfer the mixture to a greased loaf tin. With a wet spoon, press down
the dough and smooth the top. Dust the top with plain white flour and
leave to prove until the dough has risen to about 5mm (⅛in) above the
top of the tin. Preheat the oven to 190°C/375°F/Gas 5.

Bake for about 1 hour. Remove the loaf from the oven and transfer
to a cooling rack for at least 1 hour before slicing.

SPONGE
125g (4½oz) Painswick starter
  (*see page 177*)
165g (5¾oz) dark rye flour
14g (½oz) fresh yeast or 7g (¼oz)
  fast-action dried yeast
110ml (3¾fl oz) warm water

DOUGH
165g (5¾oz) dark rye flour
2 tsp black treacle
1½ tsp sea salt
110ml (3¾fl oz) warm water

Plain white flour (for dusting)

EQUIPMENT
500g/1lb loaf tin

Why not try ...
using a light rye flour if you find this
rye too heavy.

WALNUT & FIG LOAF

Makes 1 large loaf

400g (14oz) strong white flour

100g (3½oz) dark rye flour

3 tsp sea salt

40g (1½oz) honey

14g (½oz) fresh yeast or 3.5g (⅛oz) fast-action dried yeast

200ml (7fl oz) warm water

400g (14oz) Painswick starter (*see page 177*)

80g (2¾oz) walnuts, roughly chopped

80g (2¾oz) dried figs, roughly chopped

1 ice cube

EQUIPMENT

1kg/2lb loaf tin

This loaf comes from our Painswick dough. We wanted to create a loaf with texture and sweetness that our customers could serve on a cheese board. The starter used in the Painswick dough base gives the bread depth of flavour; however, you'll find the nuts and fruit overtake the tea flavour to form their own. Absolutely delicious! If you don't have a Painswick starter, or prefer a non-tea option, you could use a rye starter.

Grease a loaf tin or a large proving basket.

Put the strong white and rye flour into a bowl, then on one side add the sea salt and honey and on the other add the yeast; they shouldn't be in direct contact. Add the warm water and the Painswick or rye starter, mix all the ingredients together to form a dough, then knead for 7–10 minutes (*see Basic Techniques, page 28*). Add the walnuts and figs and knead again until well distributed. Place the dough in the loaf tin or proving basket and leave to prove until it has risen to about 2cm (¾in) above the height of the container. This takes 2–3 hours depending on room temperature. Preheat the oven to 200°C/400°F/Gas 6.

If you're using a proving basket, transfer the dough to a greased baking tray lined with baking paper. Put the loaf in the oven, on the middle shelf, then throw an ice cube to the back of the oven to create steam. Bake for 55 minutes.

Remove the loaf and leave to cool on a wire rack for 1 hour before slicing.

Why not try ...
replacing the walnuts with pecan nuts or hazelnuts, and using dried apricots or prunes instead of the figs.

SOURDOUGH

Sourdough is a very popular loaf because of its strength of flavour and slight acidic notes. When I worked as a pastry chef in London, one of my bosses once walked into the kitchen with litres of apple juice left over from a function. He asked me to make something with it, to save it going to waste. At the time, I had a reasonably young sourdough starter – just three years old. I was sure that by adding the apple juice to my dough it would help emphasize the flavour. It worked and it has been my secret sourdough ingredient ever since! I recommend using the best apple juice you can afford; the purer and fresher, the better.

200g (7oz) strong white flour
80g (2¾oz) wholemeal flour
7g (¼oz) fresh yeast or 3.5g (⅛oz)
  fast-action dried yeast
1½ tsp salt
150ml (5fl oz) apple juice
150 g (5oz) sourdough starter
  (*see page 177*)

EQUIPMENT
Proving basket

Place all the ingredients in a large bowl, bring together and knead for 7 minutes (*see Basic Techniques, page 28*). Put the dough in a large bowl, cover with clingfilm and leave to prove in the fridge overnight.

NEXT DAY

The next morning, take the dough out of the fridge and dust your proving basket with flour. Flatten the dough into a rectangle, then fold in 3–4cm (1¼–1½in) at either end. Fold the dough towards you so that the edges meet (rather like an envelope), then use the heel of your palm to press the dough so that the ends stick down. Place the dough in the proving basket, smooth side down, and dust with more flour. Leave to prove at room temperature for 1½–2 hours, until the dough has risen to 2–3cm (¾–1¼in) above the rim of the basket.

Preheat the oven to 220°C/430°F/Gas 7. Grease a baking sheet and line with baking paper.

Carefully remove the dough from the proving basket, taking care to maintain the shape, and place it on the prepared baking sheet. Slash the top using a knife with a serrated edge. Bake for 30 minutes or until golden brown.

Transfer the loaf to a wire rack and leave to cool for 40 minutes before serving.

> **Why not try ...**
> using a 50:50 white to brown flour mix, or a 100 per cent white loaf? You could use any strong bread flour.

▶ *key stages illustrated overleaf*

SOURDOUGH KEY STAGES

1. Dust the proving basket with flour.

2. Flatten the dough into a rectangle and fold in the ends.

3. Fold the dough towards you so that the edges meet.

4. Place the dough in the proving basket, smooth side down.

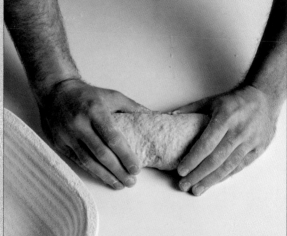

5. Dust the dough with flour and leave to prove at room temperature.

NELSON LOAF

70g (2¼oz) strong white flour
70g (2¼oz) wholemeal flour
1½ tsp baking powder
1½ tsp sea salt
50g (1¾oz) jumbo oats
25g (⅞oz) poppy seeds
25g (⅞oz) sesame seeds
25g (⅞oz) flax seeds
30g (1oz) sunflower seeds
30g (1oz) pumpkin seeds
15g (½oz) nigella seeds
230g (8oz) yogurt
70g (2¼oz) golden syrup
20g (⅔oz) vegetable oil

EQUIPMENT
500g/1lb loaf tin

I once did some work experience with a South African pastry chef in London. He inspired me by his use of seeds and oats in his bread, which he taught me was commonplace in South Africa. When I set up my bakery in 2012, I created this loaf, the majority of which is seeds and oats; it's yeast free and very easy to make. I named it after Nelson Mandela.

Serve with smoked salmon and cream cheese, or spread lightly with butter to accompany a freshly made tomato soup.

Preheat the oven to 160°C/320°F/Gas 3. Put all the ingredients into a large bowl and mix until well combined. Transfer the mixture to a greased loaf tin and, using a wet spoon, press down and smooth the top.

Bake for 1 hour, or until a cocktail stick inserted into the centre comes out clean. Carefully turn out the loaf onto a wire rack and leave to cool for 1 hour before slicing.

CIABATTA

I spend a lot of time hunting out new ideas (or sometimes old ideas done well) from books, talking to experts I know and researching ingredients and techniques online. This recipe came out of one of those hunts, when I was looking for a ciabatta loaf which was easy to make. In this recipe, all the ingredients are thrown in together, which is what makes it so simple. However, it isn't one to be made by hand; it will require an electric dough mixer. In 2014, I won Silver at the World Bread Awards for this loaf. It's perfect for a meze board or with soup, and is also ideal for making panini.

Makes 2 ciabattas

500g (1lb 2oz) strong white flour
20g (⅔oz) yeast
2 tsp sea salt
475ml (16fl oz) water

EQUIPMENT
electric dough mixer

Place all the ingredients in the bowl of your electric dough mixer. Using a dough hook, knead at high speed until the dough comes clean away from the sides of the mixing bowl. This will take about 30 minutes. Alternatively, mix and knead the dough by hand (*see Basic Techniques, page 28*).

Put the dough in a warm place and leave to prove until doubled in volume. This should take 1–1½ hours.

Scrape the dough onto a work surface dusted liberally with flour. Divide the dough into two 450g (1lb) pieces and, with well-floured hands, shape the dough into ciabatta shapes. Leave to prove again for 10–15 minutes.

Preheat the oven to 220°C/430°F/Gas 7 and grease a baking tray.

Bake for 20–25 minutes, or until golden brown on top.

Why not try ...
replacing 100g (3½oz) of the white flour with wholemeal flour to create a wholemeal ciabatta.

PAINSWICK LOAF

5g (⅙oz) Earl Grey tea leaves

100ml (3½fl oz) boiling water

50g (1¾oz) dark rye flour

200g (7oz) strong white flour

7g (¼oz) sea salt

20g (⅔oz) honey

7g (¼oz) fresh yeast or 3.5g (⅛oz)
  fast-action yeast

200g (7oz) Painswick starter
  (see page 177)

1 ice cube

EQUIPMENT

500g/1lb loaf tin

When we moved to Painswick in Gloucestershire, I wanted to create a loaf which paid homage to this beautiful village. I dug around to find out interesting bits of history and was delighted to learn that Mr Twining was born and spent much of his childhood here, many years before setting up his tea empire in London. What else could I make other than a tea-infused loaf! This recipe uses a 'starter' or 'culture' as its base. The starter takes a couple of days to make initially, but it's well worth the time and effort, as once made you can use it over and over again for years (see page 177).

Pour the boiling water into a teapot with the tea leaves and leave to brew for 10 minutes before straining.

While the tea is brewing, put the rye and white flour into a bowl. Add the sea salt and honey to one side of the bowl, placing the yeast on the other side of the bowl so it's not in direct contact with the honey or salt.

Add the Painswick starter and the infused tea, then bring the dough together with your hand or a dough scraper. Knead the dough mixture for 7 minutes.

Place in a greased loaf tin and leave to prove until the dough rises up from the top of the tin by about 2cm (¾in). This will take 1–2 hours, dependng on the temperature of the room.

Preheat the oven to 200°C/400°F/Gas 6. Place the loaf on the middle shelf and bake for 55 minutes. (To create steam in the oven while the bread is cooking, throw an ice cube to the back of the oven just after you put the loaf in; the steam helps the bread to rise to its full potential without forming a crust too early.)

Remove from the oven and allow to cool on a wire rack for 30 minutes before slicing.

Why not try …
using lapsang souchong tea instead of the Earl Grey to add a smokiness to the loaf.

WILD GARLIC TEAR-AND-SHARE

It's traditional for Jewish Israeli families to share dinner on a Friday evening. When I was a teenager, my sisters and I had to be home to eat dinner as a family before heading out to whichever party we were going to! The tradition of 'the breaking of bread', the meaning of which extends to sharing a meal, is a strong part of what I believe food should be about. This tear-and-share loaf is exactly as its name describes, and is a firm favourite of mine when sharing a meal with friends or family. You can fill it with a host of different flavours – here is my wild garlic version.

660g (1lb 7oz) strong white flour
420ml (14fl oz) warm water
14g (½oz) sea salt
14g (½oz) caster sugar
8g (¼oz) fresh yeast or 1 tsp
  fast-action dried yeast
100–150g (3½–5oz) wild garlic pesto
  (see page 178)

EQUIPMENT
cake ring

Place all the ingredients in a large bowl and combine to form a dough (*see Basic Techniques, page 28*). Knead on a cool surface for 7 minutes, then transfer to a large bowl, cover and leave to prove at room temperature until the dough has doubled in size.

Line your cake ring with baking paper.

Flatten the dough and roll out into a large rectangle about 1cm (⅓in) thick. Spread a thick layer of wild garlic pesto over the dough, then roll up the dough like a Swiss roll and cut into slices. Lay out the portions in the prepared cake ring – they should be just touching. Cover and leave to prove for 15–20 minutes.

Preheat the oven to 230°C/450°F/Gas 8. Bake for 30–35 minutes, or until golden brown on top.

Remove from the oven and place on a cooling rack for 20 minutes before serving.

Why not try ...
using sun-dried tomato paste, red pepper pesto or olive tapenade instead of the wild garlic pesto.

▶ *key stages illustrated overleaf*

WILD GARLIC TEAR-AND-SHARE KEY STAGES

1. Flatten the dough and shape into a large rectangle using a rolling pin.

2. Spread wild garlic pesto over the dough.

3. Roll up the dough like a Swiss roll.

4. Cut the dough into slices.

5. Place the slices in a cake ring so that they're just touching.

SODA BREAD

560g (1¼lb) strong white flour
1 tsp bicarbonate of soda
1 tsp sea salt
480g (16¼oz) yogurt

A few years ago when I was working in a restaurant in London, it was two hours before service, I went to check my bread dough and it hadn't risen … every pastry chef's worst nightmare! I needed a loaf quickly and this soda bread recipe came to my rescue. As there is no yeast, and therefore no proving, it's the easiest to prepare and quickest to bake – you can make this loaf within an hour. This is a super-versatile recipe – you can change the flour or try adding seeds, nuts, olives or herbs …

Preheat the oven to 180°C/350°F/Gas 4. Grease a baking tray and line with baking paper.

Put all the ingredients into a bowl and mix until they form a dough. Place the dough on a baking tray and slash the top of the dough with an 'X' shape.

Bake for 70–80 minutes, then transfer to a cooling rack and leave to cool for 1 hour before serving.

Why not try …
replacing 100g (3½oz) of white flour with wholemeal flour and using 100ml (3½fl oz) of dark beer instead of 100g (3½oz) of the yogurt, to make a darker soda bread that's full of flavour.

BANANA & PECAN SPELT LOAF

Spelt is the most ancient grain there is. It is wheat free and is believed to be a healthier, more easily digestible choice for bread. It comes in both white and wholemeal forms, just like standard flour.

I used spelt to create this perfect breakfast loaf. Add butter and jam and serve with a steaming-hot coffee. What more can I say?

200ml (7fl oz) cold water
330g (11½oz) wholemeal spelt
4g (⅛oz) fresh yeast or ¾ tsp
  fast-action dried yeast
1½ tsp salt
75g (2½oz) pecan nuts, chopped
75g (2½oz) dried cranberries
75g (2½oz) banana chips,
  roughly chopped
ground rice or flour (for dusting)

Place the water, spelt, yeast and salt in a large bowl and combine to form a dough. Place the dough on a lightly dusted work surface and knead for 10 minutes (*see Basic Techniques, page 28*). Add the chopped pecan nuts, dried cranberries and banana chips and continue kneading until well distributed. Place the dough in a large bowl, cover and leave to prove until it has doubled in size.

Shape the bread into a long, thin loaf and dust with ground rice or flour. Make slashes across the length of the dough and leave to prove for 10–15 minutes. Preheat the oven to 230°C/450°F/Gas 8.

Bake the loaf for about 30 minutes, until it looks crisp on the outside and the base sounds hollow when tapped. Place on a wire rack and leave to cool for 30 minutes before serving.

Why not try ...
using a 50:50 ratio of white and wholemeal flour if you're unable to find spelt. Or, use dried apricots and hazelnuts instead of banana and pecan nuts.

NAAN BREAD

Makes 4 naans

250g (9oz) strong white flour
50g (1¾oz) yogurt
125ml (4½fl oz) water
2½ tsp caster sugar
¼ tsp bicarbonate of soda
½ tsp baking powder
½ tsp coriander, finely chopped
½ tsp mint, finely chopped
½ tsp coriander seeds
½ tsp fennel seeds
1 tsp salt
a little oil (for frying)

This is one of the basics of bread-making for any pastry chef. It's quick and easy to make and so delicious. I made naan bread regularly when working as a pastry chef in London. It would usually accompany Indian canapés or an Indian-inspired dish for the evening. You can play around with the quantities of mint and coriander (leaves and seeds) to your liking.

Preheat the oven to 180°C/350°F/Gas 4. Mix together all the ingredients – there's no need to knead! Divide the dough into four equal pieces, then roll into oval shapes, to a thickness of about 5mm (⅛in).

Heat a little oil in a frying pan (enough to cover the bottom of the pan) and fry each naan on both sides until light golden brown. Put them in the oven for 5 minutes to finish them off.

Why not try ...
adding lightly toasted desiccated coconut and orange zest, instead of the seeds, for a sweeter finish.

JERUSALEM BAGELS

As a child, if we visited the old city area of Jerusalem on a school trip or with family, the first thing we'd look out for was a man with a donkey pulling a green cart. The cart was heaped with freshly made bagels, which we just loved. With every bagel came a small newpaper wrap, filled with the Middle Eastern herb Za'atar to dip the bagel in. I hope you enjoy these Jerualem bagels as much as I have!

Makes 10 bagels

450g (1lb) strong white flour
150g (5oz) wholemeal flour
350ml (12fl oz) water
35g (1¼oz) caster sugar
25g (⅞oz) fresh yeast or 2 x 7g
  sachets of fast-action dried yeast
2 tbsp milk
40ml (1⅓fl oz) vegetable oil
1 tsp salt
1 egg (for washing)
sesame seeds (for sprinkling)

In a large mixing bowl, place the strong white and wholemeal flour, water, sugar, yeast, milk, oil and salt. Mix together and knead for 7–10 minutes (*see Basic Techniques, page 28*). Cover the bowl and leave to prove for 1 hour, or until the dough has doubled in size.

Place the dough on a lightly floured work surface and divide into 120g (4¼oz) pieces. Shape them into bread rolls and leave to rest on the worktop for 10 minutes.

Line a baking sheet with baking paper. Using your fingers, make a hole in the middle of each bread roll and carefully stretch the dough, gradually making the hole bigger, until you have a bagel shape.

Lay the bagels on the lined baking sheet, then brush the tops with egg wash and sprinkle with sesame seeds. Leave to prove for 20–30 minutes. Preheat the oven to 180°C/350°F/Gas 4.

Bake for 15–20 minutes, or until the bagels have turned golden on the top. Leave to cool for 10 minutes before serving. My favourite way to enjoy them is to break the bagel and dip it in Za'atar.

> **Why not try ...**
> replacing the sesame seeds with any other seed topping of your choice.

▶ *key stages illustrated overleaf*

JERUSALEM BAGELS KEY STAGES

1. Use your fingers to make a hole in the middle of each roll.

2. Carefully stretch the dough to make the hole bigger.

3. Brush the tops with egg wash.

4. Sprinkle with sesame seeds.

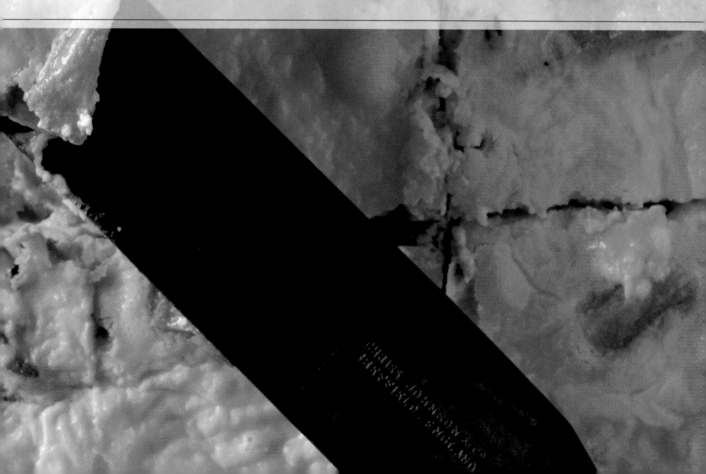

SAVOURIES

AUBERGINE & FETA TRIANGLES

I love Middle Eastern meze, and my favourite place in the world to eat it is a small restaurant in Nazareth, in the north of Israel, called Diana. I took my wife there on her first trip to Israel and she couldn't believe her eyes … no fewer then seventeen meze dishes, before we even got to the main course!

This recipe is my version of one of those wonderful dishes.

Preheat the oven to 180°C/350°F/Gas 4. Place the dough ingredients in a large bowl and mix to bring together (*see Basic Techniques, page 28*) – no kneading is required. Cover and leave to prove for 1 hour.

To make the filling, place the aubergine on a roasting tray, drizzle with plenty of olive oil and sprinkle with sea salt. Roast in the oven for 30–40 minutes or until cooked through. Remove from the oven and leave to cool completely.

Transfer the aubergine to a large bowl and add the feta cheese and the mint, then stir to mix everything together. Season to taste if necessary. Increase the oven temperature to 200°C/400°F/Gas 6.

Roll out the dough on a floured surface, to a thickness of 5mm (⅛in). Cut into circles using the 10cm (4in) pastry cutter and spoon some of the filling into the centre of each one. Bring the sides of the dough together over the top of the filling to form a triangular shape, then press together to seal. Brush with olive oil and bake for about 15 minutes or until golden brown.

Makes 20 triangles

DOUGH

300g (11oz) plain flour
1 tsp salt
120ml (4fl oz) water
2 tbsp vegetable oil
2 tbsp milk
10g (⅓oz) fresh yeast or 1 tsp
   fast-action dried yeast

FILLING

1 large aubergine, chopped into
   1cm (⅓in) cubes
olive oil (for drizzling and brushing)
sea salt (for sprinkling)
250g (9oz) feta cheese, broken into
   small pieces
1 tbsp fresh mint leaves, chopped
salt and freshly ground black pepper

EQUIPMENT

10cm (4in) round pastry cutter

BEETROOT & GOAT'S CHEESE CALZONE

Makes 10 calzones

DOUGH

14g (½oz) fresh yeast or 7g (¼oz)
  fast-action dried yeast
60ml (2fl oz) milk
500g (1lb 2oz) strong white flour
100g (3½oz) baked potato flesh,
  crushed
1 tsp salt
1 tsp caster sugar
40ml (1⅓fl oz) olive oil
240ml (8fl oz) cold water
1 egg

FILLING

3 raw beetroots, peeled and chopped
  into 1 cm (⅓in) cubes
olive oil (for drizzling)
sea salt
2 tbsp fresh thyme leaves
200g (7oz) soft goat's cheese
salt and freshly ground black pepper

This popular half-moon-shaped folded pizza is traditionally stuffed with cheese, vegetables or meat. Try this slightly more sophisticated version, with strong flavours and a healthy feel.

Preheat the oven to 180°C/350°F/Gas 4. To make the dough, place all the ingredients in a large mixing bowl and bring together with your hands. Knead the dough on a floured work surface for about 7 minutes (*see Basic Techniques, page 28*), then return to the bowl, cover and leave to prove for 2 hours, or until doubled in size.

Meanwhile, make the filling. Place the beetroot on a baking tray and drizzle with plenty of olive oil, a sprinkling of sea salt and the thyme, and roast in the oven for about 30 minutes. Remove from the oven and leave to cool completely.

Using a spoon, mix the roast beetroot with the goat's cheese and season to taste if necessary. Increase the oven temperature to 220°C/430°F/Gas 7. Grease a baking tray and line with baking paper.

Divide the dough into 100g (3½oz) pieces and leave to rest on a floured work surface for 5–10 minutes. Using a rolling pin, roll out each piece into a circular shape and spoon the filling into the centre. Brush the edges with water, then carefully bring one side over the filling to make a semi-circle, then press the edges together to seal. Make sure each calzone is sealed perfectly, with no holes or tears. Place on the prepared baking tray, dust with flour and bake for 20 minutes or until golden brown on top.

Allow to cool for 5 minutes before serving.

Why not try ...
filling the calzone with a good-quality salami (chopped) and some mozzarella. You could even add a little jalapeño pepper to give it a kick!

CAULIFLOWER MONEYBAGS

Deep-fried cauliflower served with tahini sauce is a very popular dish in Israel's Middle Eastern restaurants. My dad taught me how to make it when I was a child. More recently, I started adding filo pastry to create a crunchy texture and found it worked really well.

Makes 8 moneybags

vegetable oil (for deep-frying)
1 large cauliflower, cut into large florets
juice of 2 lemons
1 tsp rock salt
1 tsp sumac
300g (11oz) filo pastry
250g (9oz) butter, melted

Pour some vegetable oil into a large deep saucepan (the pan should be three-quarters full) and heat, making sure the temperature doesn't exceed 170°C (325°F). Deep-fry the cauliflower for 5–6 minutes, until lightly golden, then remove from the pan and place on a kitchen towel to soak up any excess oil.

Squeeze the lemon juice over the cauliflower and sprinkle with the rock salt and sumac. Leave to cool completely.

Preheat the oven to 180°C/350°F/Gas 4 and grease a baking tray. Cut the filo pastry into 12cm (5in) squares; you'll need three squares per floret. Brush the first square with melted butter, then lay another sheet on top, at a 45° angle. Brush again with butter and place the third square on top, again at a 45° angle. Brush with more melted butter and place a cauliflower floret in the middle. Take all the edges of the filo pastry and bring together to cover the cauliflower; you should have a moneybag shape. Repeat with the remaining cauliflower and filo pastry squares.

Place the moneybags on the baking tray and brush with more melted butter. Bake for 12–15 minutes, or until golden brown and crispy. Serve straight away, with tahini sauce (*see page 180*).

▶ *key stages illustrated overleaf*

CAULIFLOWER MONEYBAGS KEY STAGES

1. Layer three filo pastry squares at 45° angles, brushing each sheet with melted butter.

2. Place a deep-fried cauliflower floret in the centre of the filo squares.

3. Bring together the edges of the filo pastry, covering the cauliflower.

4. Pinch to form a moneybag shape.

5. Place the cauliflower moneybags on a baking tray and brush with more melted butter.

FIG & PROSCIUTTO DANISH

Makes 12 pastries

250g (9oz) croissant dough
 (*see page 182*)

1 egg, beaten (for washing)

250g (9oz) manchego cheese,
 sliced into shavings

100g (3½oz) prosciutto

200g (7oz) fresh figs, quartered

EQUIPMENT

5–8cm (2–3in) square pastry cutter

Savoury Danishes and pastries are becoming more and more popular. This is my savoury version of the more familiar sweet Danish.

Line a large baking tray with baking paper. Roll out the dough to form a large rectangle 5mm (⅕in) thick. Use your pastry cutter to cut the dough into twelve squares. Cut the excess dough into long strips 7mm (¼in) wide. Brush the dough squares with egg wash, then place a strip of dough around the edge to form a border. Brush the borders with egg wash and place the squares on the prepared baking tray.

Put roughly 1 tablespoon of cheese into each square, then top with a slice of prosciutto and a fig quarter. Cover the tray and leave to prove for 2 hours.

Preheat the oven to 180°C/350°F/Gas 4. Bake the Danishes for 10–15 minutes, or until they're puffed up, crispy and golden on the outside.

OLIVE TAPENADE ROLL

This is a savoury version of the famous cinnamon roll. You can use a variety of different fillings; the olive tapenade gives a delicious flavour. Perfect served as an appetizer.

First, make the tapenade. Put all the ingredients in a food processor and whizz at high speed for 5 minutes or until you have a fine paste. Any unused tapenade can be stored in an airtight container in the fridge for up to 1 month, or in the freezer for 3 months.

Grease a baking tray and line with baking paper. Roll out the dough into a rectangular shape, 5mm (⅕in) thick. Spread a thick layer of olive tapenade over the dough, then roll up lengthways, like a Swiss roll, then cut into slices 1cm (⅓in) thick. Lay the slices on the baking tray, leaving a 5cm (2in) gap in between them. Cover and leave to prove for 2 hours at room temperature. Preheat the oven to 180°C/350°F/Gas 4.

Bake for 10–14 minutes, or until golden brown on top. Transfer to a wire rack and allow to cool for 20 minutes before serving.

Makes 14 servings

250g (9oz) croissant dough
(*see page 182*)
50g (1¾oz) olive tapenade
(*see below*)

OLIVE TAPENADE
300g (11oz) mixed olives
20g (⅔oz) anchovies
1 clove of garlic
1 tbsp extra virgin olive oil
juice of 1 lemon
freshly ground black pepper

Why not try ...
using wild garlic pesto instead of the tapenade, for a different savoury flavour (*see page 178*).

RED PEPPER EMPANADAS

Makes 8 empanadas

DOUGH

550g (1lb 3oz) plain white flour,
   plus extra for rolling

2 tsp salt

1 egg

200g (7oz) butter

200ml (7fl oz) water

FILLING

4 red peppers, deseeded and
   quartered

a handful of fresh thyme

a drizzle of olive oil, plus extra
   for frying

1 onion, finely chopped

salt and freshly ground black pepper

1 egg, beaten (for washing)

EQUIPMENT

12cm (5in) pastry cutter
   (or a small bowl)

After I completed my national service in 2005, I went travelling around Central America for 6 months. It was an incredible time for me, meeting people from all around the world. I particularly remember a group of Argentinian travellers who, to finance their trip, sold empanadas from large wicker baskets on buses and on the beach. It was a real delight! Here is my Mediterranean vegetarian version.

Preheat the oven to 190°C/375°F/Gas 5. Grease a baking tray and line with baking paper.

Put all the ingredients for the dough in a large bowl and mix to bring together, then stop, as there is no kneading required. Cover the dough and leave to rest in the fridge for 30 minutes.

Meanwhile, make the filling. Place the peppers in a roasting tin with the fresh thyme and drizzle over some olive oil. Put them in the oven to roast for about 20 minutes or until the edges start to brown. Heat a little olive oil in a pan and fry the onion until golden brown.

Reduce the oven temperature to 180°C/350°F/Gas 4. Put the roasted peppers and the fried onions into a food processor and whizz for 1–2 minutes or until the mixture is finely chopped. Season to taste. Leave to cool completely before assembling the empanadas.

On a lightly floured surface, roll out the dough to a thickness of about 3mm (⅛in) and cut out eight circles using a pastry cutter or the rim of a small bowl. Spoon 2 tablespoons of filling into the centre of each disc and brush the edges of the dough with water. Fold over one half of each disc to make a semicircular parcel. Press the edges together firmly, then crimp or press the edges with a fork.

Place the empanadas on the prepared baking tray and brush the tops with beaten egg. Bake for about 20 minutes or until golden brown. Leave to cool for 5 minutes before serving.

Why not try ...
replacing the red pepper filling with an aubergine and feta filling (*see Aubergine & Feta Triangles, page 83*).

SAFFRON, PINE NUT & RICOTTA QUICHE

250g (9oz) croissant dough
  (see page 182)
400ml (13½fl oz) double cream
260ml (8¾fl oz) milk
a few strands of saffron
4 eggs, plus extra for washing
2 egg yolks
salt and freshly ground black pepper
180g (6¼oz) ricotta cheese
50g (1¾oz) pine nuts, roasted

EQUIPMENT
rectangular tart tin
good-quality clingfilm
dried beans or rice

Quiche is a great dish for using up any left-over cheese and vegetables. It takes a bit of work to make, but it's well worth the effort. It's one of my favourite 'feel good' dishes.

Preheat the oven to 180°C/350°F/Gas 4. Grease the tart tin and line with baking paper.

Roll out the dough to 3mm (⅛in) thick, to the appropriate shape and size for your tart tin; the dough should be 5mm (⅛in) higher than the top of the tin. Place the dough in the tin, then cover with three layers of clingfilm. Cover the base with a layer of dried beans or rice, then blind-bake for 30–35 minutes or until the base is cooked.

Carefully remove the beans and the clingfilm, and brush the base with egg wash. Return to the oven for 2–3 minutes, to seal any holes or tears in the base. Remove and leave to cool completely.

To make the filling, put the cream, milk and saffron in a saucepan and bring to the boil, then cover, take off the stove and leave to infuse for 10 minutes. Put the eggs and the egg yolks in a large bowl. Bring the infused mixture back to the boil, then pour over the eggs and whisk together. Pass the mixture through a fine sieve, into a jug. Season with salt and pepper and set aside.

Preheat the oven to 130°C/250°F/Gas ½. Scatter the ricotta cheese and the pine nuts over the base and pour the cream mixture over the top. Carefully put the quiche in the oven and bake for 40–50 minutes, or until the top is completely set when you shake the tin.

Leave to cool completely for at least 2 hours, or overnight in the fridge, before serving.

Why not try ...
using asparagus and chorizo, for a meaty option. Cook the asparagus in boiling water for 2–3 minutes, then cut into small chunks. Slice the chorizo and fry over a moderate heat. Put them in the blind-baked pastry case and pour over the egg mixture.

PARMESAN & POPPY-SEED PUFF TWISTS

These puff-pastry twists are delicious with soup or even just as a light snack. It takes a while to master the technique of twisting the pastry to make a perfectly straight stick, but after a few attempts it does get easier.

Makes 20 puff twists

150g (5oz) Parmesan cheese, grated
25g (⅞oz) poppy seeds
250g (9oz) croissant dough
 (*see page 182*)
3 egg yolks, beaten (for brushing)

Place the Parmesan cheese and the poppy seeds in a bowl, mix well and set aside.

Roll the croissant dough into a rectangular shape, to a thickness of 3mm (⅛in). Brush with the egg yolk and sprinkle the cheese and poppy seeds evenly over the top. Place the dough on a chopping board and put in the fridge for 10 minutes. Keep any left-over cheese and poppy-seed mixture.

Preheat the oven to 180°C/350°F/Gas 4 and grease a baking tray.

Using a large knife, cut the dough into 1cm (⅓in) strips. Twist each strip, making sure the poppy seeds are on the outside. Place on the prepared baking tray, leaving space between the strips.

Bake for 10–15 minutes, or until golden brown. Leave to cool for at least 10 minutes before serving.

Why not try ...
replacing the poppy seeds with coriander or fennel seeds and adding a sprinkling of smoked paprika.

▶ *key stages illustrated overleaf*

PARMESAN & POPPY-SEED PUFF TWISTS

1. Roll out the dough to form a rectangle.

2. Brush the dough with egg yolk.

3. Sprinkle with an even coating of Parmesan cheese and poppy seeds.

4. Cut the dough into strips.

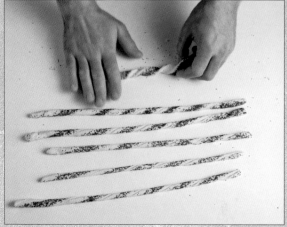

5. Twist the strips, making sure the poppy seeds are on the outside.

6. Place the strips on a baking tray, leaving space in between them.

Roasted Butternut Squash & Oregano Clafoutis

Makes 6–8 servings

500g (1lb 2oz) butternut squash, peeled, deseeded and cut into wedges
olive oil (for drizzling)
1 tsp sea salt
2 tbsp fresh oregano leaves

FILLING
400ml (13½fl oz) double cream
260ml (8¾fl oz) milk
4 eggs
2 egg yolks
salt and freshly ground black pepper

EQUIPMENT
20 x 10cm (8 x 4in) baking tin

A traditional clafoutis is a sweet French flan-based dessert that is baked in the oven; it usually contains fruit. I took inspiration from this and created a savoury version with Mediterranean flavours. It's baked without pastry, which makes it a great gluten-free option. This is a very adaptable recipe – you can be as creative as you like!

Preheat the oven to 200°C/400°F/Gas 6.

Spread out the butternut squash on a roasting tray, drizzle with plenty of olive oil and sprinkle with the sea salt. Roast in the oven for 30–35 minutes, or until cooked through.

Meanwhile, make the filling. Put the cream and milk in a saucepan and bring to the boil. Place the eggs and the egg yolks in a large bowl and pour the cream and milk over the top. Whisk the mixture, then pass through a fine sieve, into a jug. Season with salt and pepper and set aside.

Reduce the oven temperature to 130°C/250°F/Gas ½. Place the roasted butternut squash in a baking tin and sprinkle with the oregano, then pour over the filling so that the squash is covered.

Bake for 40–50 minutes, or until the top looks completely set when you shake the tin. Leave to cool for 10 minutes before serving.

Why not try …
steamed broccoli, kale and mature Cheddar cheese. You can use any vegetable or cheese in this dish.

SOURDOUGH PIZZA

The sourdough pizza base is becoming a must-have for any respectable authentic pizzeria. Here is my take on it.

Makes 2 pizzas

DAY ONE

200g (7oz) strong white flour

80g (2¾oz) wholemeal flour

7g (¼oz) yeast or 3.5g (⅛oz)
  fast-action dried yeast

1½ tsp salt

150ml (5fl oz) water

150g (5oz) sourdough starter
  (*see page 177*)

50ml (1¾fl oz) olive oil

DAY TWO

100g (3½oz) rich tomato sauce
  (*see page 178*)

2 x 125g (4½oz) mozzarella cheese
  balls, sliced

300g (11oz) artichoke hearts,
  cut into chunks

2 handfuls of rocket

EQUIPMENT

2 x 20cm (8in) baking trays

Place the flours, yeast, salt, water and sourdough starter in a large bowl, mix together and knead for 7 minutes, using an electric dough mixer or by hand (*see Basic Techniques, page 28*). Add the olive oil, increase the mixing speed, and stir until all the oil is incorporated. Loosely cover the bowl with clingfilm, and leave in the fridge overnight.

NEXT DAY

Preheat the oven to 220°C/430°F/Gas 7. Cut the dough in half, roll out each piece to form a round pizza base and place on a baking tray. Spread half of the tomato sauce over each base, add the mozzarella slices, scatter over the artichokes and finish with a handful of rocket. Bake for 20–25 minutes, or until the edges of the pizzas are golden brown.

CAKES

BROWNIES

Before I even started my training at Le Cordon Bleu, I cooked at home all the time – both savoury and sweet dishes. I was constantly on the lookout for recipes and thinking about how I could recreate them. I started making these brownies back then, and, even after many years of training and working in the industry, this is still my favourite brownie recipe. It's chocolatey and gooey in the middle ... What more could you want? It's also nut free. I make this at home as much as at work, and no one seems to get bored with it.

Makes 15 pieces

350g (12¼oz) dark chocolate
250g (9oz) butter
60ml (2fl oz) strong coffee
250g (9oz) cake flour
¼ tsp salt
1 tsp baking powder
400g (14oz) caster sugar
4 eggs
100g (3½oz) dark chocolate, chopped

EQUIPMENT
325 x 265 x 50mm (12¾ x 10½ x 2in)
  baking tray

Preheat the oven to 180°C/350°F/Gas 4. Grease the baking tray with butter or oil and line with baking paper.

Heat the chocolate, butter and coffee over a bain-marie until the chocolate and butter have melted.

Sift the flour, salt and baking powder into a bowl. Whisk the sugar and eggs until they've doubled in volume. Add the melted chocolate mixture to the eggs and sugar. Using a whisk, mix well, then add the flour mixture, folding until well combined. Lastly, fold in the chopped chocolate.

Pour the mixture into the prepared tin and, using a palette knife or scraper, level out the surface. Bake for about 30 minutes or until the top has started to crack and a cocktail stick inserted in the middle comes out clean.

Why not try ...
replacing the strong coffee with Baileys or any liquor of your choice, to give your brownies a really special flavour. Also, if you're a fan of nuts, you could add 100g (3½oz) of chopped nuts with the chopped chocolate.

BLUEBERRY & WHITE CHOCOLATE CAKES

I love using yogurt in food, especially my cakes. It gives a velvety texture and a very special sour hint to the sponge. Adding the blueberries to these cakes adds a burst of acidity that's needed to balance the flavour. This is another adult cake recipe, designed to impress!

Preheat the oven to 160°C/320°F/Gas 3.

Cream together the butter and sugar, then gradually add the eggs and vanilla, folding in gently. Gradually add batches of flour and yogurt alternately, using a spatula to gently fold in each addition. Finish with a batch of flour. Once everything is well incorporated, fold in the blueberries.

Transfer the mixture to a piping bag and pipe into the greased silicone moulds. Bake for 30–40 minutes, until a cocktail stick inserted into the centres comes out clean. Place the cakes on a wire rack to cool for 30 minutes, before icing.

To make the white chocolate ganache, heat the cream in a saucepan until it comes to the boil. Put the white chocolate pieces in a bowl, then pour the cream over the top. Leave for a minute, then, using a whisk or a hand blender, whisk until combined. Leave to cool slightly, until the mixture has thickened. If the ganache is too thick, place the bowl over hot water to melt it down again.

Dip each blueberry cake into the ganache, decorate with the strawberries (if using) and leave to set for 10–15 minutes.

Makes 17 cakes

CAKES
200g (7oz) butter
300g (11oz) caster sugar
3 eggs, room temperature
seeds of ½ vanilla pod or 1 tsp
  vanilla essence
350g (12¼oz) self-raising flour
240g (8½oz) yogurt, room temperature
200g (7oz) fresh blueberries

GANACHE
100ml (3½fl oz) single cream
200g (7oz) white chocolate, broken
  into pieces

DECORATION
freeze-dried strawberries (optional)

EQUIPMENT
silicone cupcake or muffin tray
piping bag

LEMON POLENTA CAKE

300g (11oz) caster sugar, plus extra
  for dusting
300g (11oz) butter
4 eggs
150g (5oz) polenta, finely ground
300g (11oz) ground almonds
zest of 3 lemons
35ml (1¼fl oz) lemon juice

EQUIPMENT
deep round 23cm (9in) spring-release
  cake tin

This cake has a great texture, is full of flavour and is popular with everyone, not just those who need to choose a gluten-free option. It's citrusy, light and sweet. For me, this is a guilt-free choice – unless, of course, you start adding crème fraîche …

Preheat the oven to 140°C/275°F/Gas 1. Line your cake tin with baking paper.

Using an electric mixer, cream together the sugar and butter until the mixture is pale and has increased in volume. Add the eggs one at a time, adding some of the polenta in between each egg until it's all incorporated. Add the ground almonds and mix briefly, then add the lemon zest and juice and fold in with a spatula. Pour the batter into the prepared tin and level out the top.

Bake for about 1 hour, until a cocktail stick inserted into the centre comes out clean. Dust the top with caster sugar, then leave to cool completely.

Release the cake from the tin carefully, as it will be very fragile.

Why not try …
making an orange-flavoured version of the cake by using orange juice and zest instead of lemon.

NUTELLA BRIOCHE

When I teach this in my classes, there is often an air of scepticism over how chocolate spread can make such a great bake, but my students are always won around by how delicious these Nutella brioches look and taste. It's one of the bakes they recreate most often at home. These little brioches are a perfect treat for a family gathering, and a tasty alternative to cupcakes or brownies. Adults love them as much as kids! The dough needs to prove overnight, but don't be put off by the two-day process – it's worth the wait.

Makes 30 brioches

DAY ONE
550g (1lb 3oz) strong white flour
20g (⅔oz) fresh yeast or 10g (⅓oz)
　fast-action yeast
75g (2½oz) caster sugar
125ml (4½fl oz) milk
12g (½oz) salt
4 eggs
125g (4½oz) butter, softened

DAY TWO
large jar of Nutella (1 tbsp per brioche)
egg yolk (for washing)

EQUIPMENT
2 mini-muffin trays

Place the flour, yeast, sugar, milk and salt in a large bowl and mix together. Crack in the eggs and continue to mix (using your hand or a flexible dough scraper) until the dough starts to form.

Knead the dough mixture for about 7 minutes, then add the softened butter and continue kneading until all the butter is incorporated. Cover the dough lightly with clingfilm and leave it in the fridge to prove overnight.

NEXT DAY
Divide the dough into 30 equal pieces by rolling it into a sausage shape so you can cut off even-sized chunks. If you want to be really precise, you can weigh each piece (about 30g/1oz each).

One at a time, roll out each dough piece into a circular shape. Place one tablespoon of Nutella in the centre of each circle.

Fold the dough over the Nutella to form a semi-circle, and seal it by pressing around the rim of the semi-circle with your fingers. Push together both ends of the dough to form a 'stalk', ensuring that all the Nutella is in the round shape that forms at the top. The bun shape should now loosely resemble a mushroom.

Place the filled buns into a muffin tray as you go, then brush the tops lightly with egg yolk. Leave to prove in a warm place for about 1 hour, or until increased in volume to about one and a half times the size.

Preheat the oven to 180°C/350°F/Gas 4 and bake for 10–12 minutes until golden. Enjoy warm, fresh from the oven. (If you want to reheat them later, place in a preheated oven for 3 minutes, or heat in the microwave for about 20 seconds.)

Why not try ...
experimenting with different fillings – just make sure you choose something that holds its shape when spooned onto the rolled-out dough. Peanut butter or crème patissière (*see recipe on page 181*) are good alternatives, as are hazelnut praline or dark chocolate ganache.

▶ *key stages illustrated overleaf*

NUTELLA BRIOCHE KEY STAGES

1. Roll out the pieces of dough into rough circles.

2. Place a tablespoon of Nutella into the centre of each piece of dough.

3. Fold the dough over the Nutella and seal the edges with your fingers.

4. Push the ends of the dough together to make a stalk, forming a mushroom shape.

5. Place the 'mushrooms' in the muffin tray, stalk side down, and brush the tops with egg yolk.

FRUITS OF THE FOREST MUFFINS

A few years ago I set out to create a healthy muffin recipe – one that you'd be happy to give your children for breakfast. This recipe uses wholemeal flour, oats and berries and contains no butter. It's a firm favourite with my two-year-old!

Makes 10 muffins

200g (7oz) light brown sugar
2 eggs
180ml (6fl oz) milk
120ml (4¼fl oz) vegetable oil
280g (10 oz) wholemeal flour
2 tsp baking powder
½ tsp salt
100g (3½oz) oats
120g (4¼oz) mixed berry fruits

EQUIPMENT
large muffin tray
10 paper muffin cases
piping bag

Preheat the oven to 170°C/325°F/Gas 3. Line the muffin tray with paper cases.

Put the sugar, eggs, milk and oil in a large bowl and whisk gently until well combined. Sift the flour, baking powder and salt into a second bowl, then add to the sugar and egg mixture in three stages, using the whisk to fold the ingredients in gently. Once everything is well combined, fold in the oats and mixed berries.

Transfer the mixture to a piping bag and pipe into the muffin cases. Bake for about 30 minutes, or until a cocktail stick inserted into the centres comes out clean.

Place the muffins on a wire rack and leave to cool for about 30 minutes before serving. They will keep in the freezer for up to 3 months.

MUM'S YOGURT CAKE

I get my love of food, and especially baking, from my mum. The first cake she ever taught me to bake was this yogurt cake. I was six years old and I was fiercely independent, insisting she allow me to make it time and time again, weighing and mixing all on my own. My favourite part was pouring the hot lemon syrup over the top of the cake and watching how it was all absorbed by the sponge. It's still one of my favourite bakes.

225g (8oz) cake flour
2 tsp baking powder
½ tsp salt
225g (8oz) caster sugar
15g (½oz) lemon zest
120g (4¼oz) oil
2 eggs
seeds of ½ vanilla pod
180g (6¼oz) yogurt

SYRUP
360ml (12fl oz) water
150g (5oz) caster sugar
2½ tbsp lemon juice

EQUIPMENT
500g/1lb loaf tin

Preheat the oven to 160°C/320°F/Gas 3. Grease the loaf tin.

Sieve the flour, baking powder and salt into a bowl and set aside. Put the sugar and lemon zest into a second bowl, then, in a third bowl whisk together the oil, eggs, vanilla seeds and yogurt. Add the sugar and lemon and fold in, followed by the flour, baking powder and salt.

Pour the batter into your prepared tin, then bake for 45–50 minutes, or until the top is golden brown and a thin skewer inserted into the centre comes out clean.

While the cake is baking, make the syrup. Put all the ingredients into a saucepan and bring to the boil, then simmer for 2–3 minutes. Take care not to let the syrup caramelize, as it will be too thick to soak into the cake.

Remove the cake from the oven and, while it's still in the tin, pour the hot syrup over the top. Leave the cake to cool in the tin for 30 minutes, to allow the syrup to soak into the cake. Then transfer to a wire rack and leave for another 30 minutes to cool completely.

Gluten-free Chocolate Cakes

Makes 12 individual cakes

CAKES
250g (9oz) dark chocolate
250g (9oz) unsalted butter
5 eggs
5 egg yolks
135g (4¾oz) caster sugar
25g (⅞oz) cornflour

GANACHE
125g (4½oz) double cream
125g (4½oz) dark chocolate, broken
 into pieces

DECORATION
white chocolate, chopped

EQUIPMENT
12-hole silicone muffin tray or muffin tin
piping bag

Whenever I have a request for gluten-free cakes, I immediately pull this one from my recipe book. These cakes are deliciously rich and addictive, with a good amount of quality dark chocolate. You could never tell that they're made with cornflour!

Preheat the oven to 180°C/350°F/Gas 4. If using a muffin tin, grease with butter or oil.

First, make the cakes. Put the dark chocolate and unsalted butter in a bain-marie and heat until melted.

Put the eggs, egg yolks and sugar in a large bowl and whisk for 3–4 minutes. Add the melted chocolate and butter and fold through the egg mixture using your whisk. Finally, add the cornflour and fold into the mixture.

Spoon the cake batter into a piping bag and pipe into the muffin moulds, leaving a 5mm (⅕in) gap at the top. Bake for about 30 minutes, or until a cocktail stick inserted in the middle comes out clean.

Transfer the cakes to a wire rack and leave to cool for about 30 minutes, before icing.

To make the ganache, pour the cream into a small saucepan and bring to the boil. Put the chocolate in a large bowl and pour the cream over the top. Leave to stand for 1 minute, then mix with a hand blender.

Dip the chocolate cakes into the ganache and leave to set for 2 minutes, then sprinkle chopped white chocolate over the top.

Raspberry Blondies

A couple of years ago when I set up my own business, I was seeking inspiration for a new and different bake. It had to be easy to make in large quantities, without compromising on taste. That's when I came across the blondie: a white chocolate version of a brownie. I added raspberries to give it a twist and topped it with white chocolate ganache ... heaven!

These blondies are delicious as they come, but if you want to top yours with ganache too, use the recipe included for Blueberry & White Chocolate Cakes on page 113.

Makes 15 pieces

250g (9oz) butter
350g (12¼oz) white chocolate
400g (14oz) caster sugar
250g (9oz) cake flour
4 eggs
150g (5oz) fresh raspberries

EQUIPMENT
325 x 265 x 50mm (12¾ x 10½ x 2in)
  baking tray

Preheat the oven to 140°C/275°F/Gas 1. Line your baking tray with greaseproof paper.

Gently melt the butter in a saucepan or a microwave. Place the white chocolate in a large bowl and pour the hot melted butter over the top. Using a spatula, mix until well combined. Add the sugar and flour in three stages; in between each stage, add some of the egg. To finish, fold in the raspberries.

Transfer the mixture to the prepared tin. Smooth the surface and bake for 70 minutes, or until lightly golden on top. Leave to cool completely before cutting into squares. (If topping with white chocolate ganache, dip each square into the slightly cooled ganache mixture and leave to set for 10–15 minutes before eating.)

Why not try ...
using other berries instead of raspberries; pitted cherries, blackberries or mixed berries will all produce a great result. Or, for a nutty texture, try halving the quantity of berries and replacing with chopped almonds or hazelnuts.

Olive Oil & Rosemary Cakes

Makes 8 individual cakes

CAKES

100g (3½oz) wholemeal flour
100g (3½oz) cake flour
1 tsp baking powder
½ tsp salt
4 eggs
150g (5oz) light brown sugar
130ml (4½fl oz) olive oil
30g (1oz) rosemary, finely chopped

GANACHE

100ml (3½fl oz) single cream
200g (7oz) white chocolate, broken
  into pieces

EQUIPMENT

8 mini loaf tins

When I worked as a pastry chef in fine dining restaurants, I'd make this recipe as part of the cake selection for afternoon tea. It's a sophisticated cake with a unique flavour. The olive oil makes it smooth and moist, while the rosemary provides a kick. It tastes completely different to anything else, and you'll want to eat more …

Preheat the oven to 160°C/320°F/Gas 3. Sift the wholemeal and cake flour, baking powder and salt into a large bowl. Whisk the eggs and sugar until pale and increased in volume, then gradually add the olive oil. Add the flour mixture and stir to combine. Once well incorporated, add the rosemary and fold in gently.

Spoon the mixture into the loaf tins and bake for 20–25 minutes, until a cocktail stick inserted in the middle comes out clean. Leave to cool on a wire rack for about 30 minutes.

To make the white chocolate ganache, put the cream in a saucepan and bring to the boil. Put the white chocolate in a bowl, then pour the cream over the top. Leave for a minute; then, using a whisk or a hand blender, beat until well combined. Leave to cool down slightly, until the mixture has thickened. If the ganache is too thick, place the bowl over hot water to melt it down again.

Use a palette knife to spread the ganache over the top of the cake. Leave to set for 10–15 minutes before serving.

PISTACHIO & ROSE CAKES

These are cakes that I often made when working in London, and I brought them with me to the Cotswolds, where they're still a firm favourite among my customers. The pistachio flavour comes from 100 per cent raw pistachios and is complemented by rose water. This really is one to impress your guests with!

Preheat the oven to 160°C/320°F/Gas 3.

Sift the ground almonds and self-raising flour into a large bowl. Cream together the butter and sugar until they've turned pale, then add the pistachio paste and fold into the mixture. Fold in the eggs and the flour mixture a little at a time, finishing with the flour. Using a piping bag, pipe the batter into the greased moulds, and bake for 20–30 minutes depending on size.

Remove the cakes from the oven and leave to cool on a wire rack for an hour, before icing.

To make the icing, whisk together the icing sugar, rose water and a splash of cold water, adjusting the consistency if necessary. If it's too thick, add a little more water; if it's too runny, add more icing sugar. The icing should pour very slowly.

Spoon the icing over the cakes. If you wish, you could decorate them with crystallized rose petals (*see page 181*).

▶ *key stages illustrated overleaf*

Makes 12 individual cakes

CAKES

50g (1¾oz) ground almonds
150g (5oz) self-raising flour
150g (5oz) butter, softened
200g (7oz) caster sugar
70g (2¼oz) pistachio paste
  (*see page 180*)
4 eggs, room temperature

ICING

250g (9oz) icing sugar
a few drops of rose water
a little cold water

EQUIPMENT

muffin tray or mini Bundt cake pan
piping bag

Why not try ...
replacing the pistachio paste with any other nut paste. The amount of oil required may vary, so add the oil very gradually, until you have a paste consistency.

PISTACHIO & ROSE CAKES KEY STAGES

1. Cream together the butter and sugar until they turn pale.

2. Add the pistachio paste.

3. Add the eggs and the flour mixture, a little at a time.

4. Ensure that all the ingredients are incorporated.

5. Using a piping bag, pipe the batter into the cake moulds.

PANETTONE

The word 'panettone' derives from the Italian word 'panetto' – a small loaf cake. Every year, 1 November is the beginning of panettone season in my kitchen. My panettones are individually sized, which prevents the staling and wastage that you often get with large ones. They are a great alternative to mince pies and are delicious all year round! Eat warm and fresh from the oven.

Makes 12 panettones

25g (⅞oz) fresh yeast or 2½ tsp
   fast-action dried yeast
240ml (8fl oz) warm water
1 vanilla pod
1½ tsp orange compound or orange
   blossom water
85g (3oz) icing sugar
3 egg yolks
1½ tsp salt
610g (1lb 6oz) strong white flour
110g (scant 4oz) butter, softened
85g (3oz) sultanas
55g (1¾oz) candied orange
1 egg, beaten (for brushing)

EQUIPMENT
deep 12-hole muffin tray

Dissolve the yeast in the warm water, then scrape in the seeds from the vanilla pod and add the orange compound or blossom water.

In a mixing bowl, beat the icing sugar into the egg yolks. Add the salt and a handful of the flour. Add the yeast mixture, stirring with a wooden spoon to combine. Add the remaining flour a little at a time, until the mixture forms a dough.

Knead the dough for about 7 minutes, until it has an elastic consistency. Then, add the softened butter and knead again until it's well incorporated. Add the sultanas and candied orange, and knead for another 2 minutes, until well distributed. Leave the dough to prove at room temperature, until it has doubled in size (about 2 hours). Grease your muffin tray with butter or oil.

Cut the dough into 100g (3½oz) pieces and form into bread-roll shapes (*see page 31*). Place them in the greased muffin moulds, then brush the tops with egg wash. Leave to prove in a warm place, until the tops have increased in size by 150 per cent. Preheat the oven to 180°C/350°F/Gas 4.

Bake the panettones for 25–30 minutes, until they are golden brown and can be removed from the moulds easily. Transfer to a wire rack and leave to cool for 10 minutes before serving.

Why not try ...
replacing the fruit with the same quantity of chopped chocolate or chocolate chips.

SOMETHING WITH
YOUR COFFEE

BISCOTTI

I used to make a larger version of these biscotti, to accompany ice cream, but these smaller ones are ideal to enjoy with your after-dinner coffee. I like to use lots of dried fruit and green pistachios to give them a vibrant, textured appearance. Biscotti should be crunchy, and the key to achieving this crunch is to dry them out slowly using a cool oven.

Makes about 50 biscotti

170g (6oz) plain white flour
1 tsp baking powder
20g (⅔oz) ground almonds
90g (3¼oz) caster sugar
2 eggs
50g (1¾oz) pistachios, peeled
   (to give them their green colour)
50g (1¾oz) dried apricots, chopped
50g (1¾oz) dried figs, chopped
zest of 1 orange
zest of 1 lemon

EQUIPMENT
2 x 30cm (12in) loaf tins

Grease the loaf tins with butter or oil.

Sift the flour and baking powder into a large bowl and add the ground almonds and the sugar. Add the eggs and mix with a plastic scraper or with your hands. Once everything is combined, add the pistachios, dried fruit and orange and lemon zests. Fold in to combine. Preheat the oven to 170°C/325°F/Gas 3.

Divide the mixture into two equal portions. On a floured surface, roll the dough into two sausage shapes and transfer each one to a loaf tin. Bake for 25–30 minutes, or until the top is golden and a cocktail stick inserted into the middle comes out clean. Leave to cool completely.

Reduce the oven temperature to 110°C/225°F/Gas ¼. Line a baking tray with baking paper.

Cut the loaf into 1cm (⅓in) slices and place on the baking tray. Put the biscotti in the cool oven to toast gently for 30–45 minutes. Once cooled, put them in an airtight container. They will keep for up to 1 month.

CHOCOLATE BALLS

Makes about 20 balls

desiccated coconut (for coating)

200g (7oz) digestive biscuits, finely crushed

150g (5oz) caster sugar

75g (2½oz) cocoa powder

100g (3½oz) butter, melted

1 tsp vanilla extract

180ml (6fl oz) whole milk

This is a lovely recipe for children to try. There's no baking involved (other than toasting the coconut) and everything is made and rolled by hand, which means lots of messy fun! When I was little, my two big sisters and I would make these before any family party; I loved walking round handing them out.

Preheat the oven to 180°C/350°F/Gas 4. Spread out a layer of desiccated coconut on a baking tray and toast in the oven for 6–8 minutes.

Place all the ingredients except for the coconut in a large bowl. Mix well and put in the fridge for 30 minutes to set.

Take walnut-sized pieces of the mixture and, with wet hands, roll them into balls. Put the toasted desiccated coconut in a large bowl and drop in four or five chocolate balls at a time, making sure they are well coated.

Put the chocolate balls on a tray and place in the fridge to set for at least 1 hour before serving.

CITRUS MADELEINES

Madeleines take me back to the rush and pressure of a fine-dining restaurant kitchen. Once I had sent out desserts, I'd have 10 minutes to make the madeleines to go out with coffees. I'd brush the tins with butter, pipe the pre-prepared madeleine mixture, slide them into the oven for 8 minutes – then out and onto a plate, a quick dusting of icing sugar and off they went! Hopefully, you'll enjoy making this recipe at a slightly more relaxed pace.

Makes about 30 madeleines

250g (9oz) plain flour
2 tsp baking powder
200g (7oz) caster sugar
3 eggs
75ml (2½fl oz) milk
zest of 1 lemon
zest of 1 orange
zest of 1 lime
125g (4½oz) butter, melted and cooled

EQUIPMENT
madeleine tray
piping bag

Preheat the oven to 180°C/350°F/Gas 4. Brush the madeleine moulds with softened butter.

Sift the flour and baking powder into a bowl and set aside. Put the sugar and eggs in a separate large bowl, and whisk until pale and doubled in volume. Fold in the flour and baking powder. Gradually pour in the milk, stirring as you do so, then add the zests. Finally, stir in the cooled melted butter. Transfer the mixture to a piping bag and pipe it into the moulds.

Bake for 6–8 minutes, then cut one open to make sure it's cooked in the middle. Sprinkle icing sugar over the madeleines and serve while still hot.

FLORENTINES

Makes 15 pieces

SHORTBREAD BASE
240g (8½oz) butter
125g (4½oz) icing sugar
40g (1½oz) ground almonds
2 eggs
320g (11¼oz) flour

FLORENTINE MIXTURE
60g (2oz) honey
200g (7oz) caster sugar
50ml (1¾fl oz) water
2 tsp glucose
60g (2oz) butter
40g (1½oz) single cream
200g (7oz) flaked almonds

DIPPING
milk chocolate, melted

EQUIPMENT
325 x 265 x 50mm (12¾ x 10½ x 2in)
   baking tray
palette knife

My Florentines are made with a shortbread base and sticky almonds set in caramel and are dipped in chocolate. This is a recipe I tend to use a lot in the run-up to Christmas. It's easy to make in a large flat baking tray and cut into pieces.

Heat the oven to 180°C/350°F/Gas 4. Line the baking tray with baking paper.

First, make the shortbread base. Place the butter, icing sugar and ground almonds in a large bowl and, using your hands, mix to form a breadcrumb consistency. Add the eggs and a third of the flour and stir to combine. Add the remaining flour and mix to a smooth dough. Don't overmix.

Roll out the dough on a floured surface; it should be about 3mm (⅛in) thick. Make sure it will fit into your baking tray. Using your rolling pin as a support, transfer the dough to the lined tray. Feel the dough with your hands to make sure it's an even thickness. Pierce all over with a fork. Bake for about 15 minutes, or until very light golden brown. Leave to cool.

To make the Florentine mixture, place all the ingredients apart from the flaked almonds into a large saucepan. Bring to the boil and cook for a few minutes, stirring continuously; make sure it doesn't turn to caramel. You only want the syrup to be slightly thickened. Take the pan off the heat and add the flaked almonds, stirring well to coat the almonds thoroughly.

Pour the mixture over the shortbread base and spread evenly, using a palette knife. Bake for 15–20 minutes, or until golden brown on top. Leave to cool for 10–15 minutes, then cut to your desired shape.

Dip one part of each Florentine in the melted chocolate, then leave on baking paper to set. Once cooled and hardened, they can be stored in an airtight container for up to 2 months.

DATE BAKLAVA

The ultimate 'something with your coffee' – the baklava! Growing up in Israel, our family used to visit a small Arab town called Abu Gosh, just outside Jerusalem, to eat at a local restaurant there. It was there that I became accustomed to drinking black Arabic coffee and eating baklava at the end of a meal. It was a tradition that you were expected to follow, and, if you didn't, it could be seen as rude! The owners of the restaurant are now great friends of my family, and you'll still find us all back there for special occasions.

Makes about 48 baklava

100g (3½oz) dried dates
150g (5oz) ground almonds
1 tbsp mixed spice
400g (14oz) caster sugar
200ml (7fl oz) water
50ml (1¾fl oz) lemon juice
500g (1lb 2oz) filo pastry
250g (9oz) unsalted butter, melted

EQUIPMENT
30 x 20cm (12 x 8in) high-sided baking
   tray or ovenproof dish

To make the filling, soak the dates in boiling water for 10 minutes. Strain, then put them in a food processor with the ground almonds and mixed spice. Blitz for 5 minutes, until you have a smooth, spreadable purée.

Next, make the syrup. Put the sugar, water and lemon juice in a saucepan, bring to the boil and simmer gently for 5–7 minutes, taking care not to let the syrup reduce down too much.

Preheat the oven to 180°C/350°F/Gas 4. Cut the filo pastry into a rectangle the same size as the base of your tray. Brush the baking tray with melted butter and lay the first sheet of filo pastry inside. Brush with butter and place another sheet of pastry on top. Repeat until you have ten layers of filo pastry. Spread a 2mm (1/12in) coat of the date filling over the top layer and cover with another ten sheets of pastry, in the same way as before. Brush the top with melted butter and, using a sharp knife, cut the baklava into 2cm (¾in) squares, leaving them in the tin.

Bake for 30–40 minutes, until golden brown and crispy. Remove from the oven and leave to cool completely.

Pour over the sugar syrup, then leave to soak for at least 3 hours, or overnight, before serving.

> **Why not try ...**
> replacing the date filling with 250g (9oz) of finely chopped nuts (any that you like), a teaspoon of mixed spice and 30g (1oz) of demerera sugar.

▶ *key stages illustrated overleaf*

DATE BAKLAVA KEY STAGES

1. Place ten sheets of filo pastry in a baking tray or ovenproof dish, brushing each layer with melted butter.

2. Spread some of the date filling over the tenth sheet of filo pastry.

3. Cover the filling with ten more sheets of filo pastry, and repeat.

4. Cut the baklava into squares using a sharp knife.

5. When the baklava have cooled, pour over the sugar syrup and leave to soak.

CHOCOLATE PILLOWS

Makes about 20 cookies

340g (12oz) dark chocolate, broken
   into pieces
55g (1¾oz) butter
3 eggs
100g (3½oz) caster sugar (plus extra
   for dipping)
40ml (1⅓fl oz) Grand Marnier
100g (3½oz) strong white flour
½ tsp baking powder
110g (scant 4oz) ground almonds
icing sugar (for dipping)

I love the look of these chocolate pillows on a plate, the icing sugar sprinkled over the cracked top of the cookies. The Grand Marnier adds an orange kick.

Put the chocolate and butter in a saucepan and heat, stirring regularly, until melted. Keep warm.

Using an electric whisk, whip the eggs and sugar until thick and the mixture leaves a trail when you lift the whisk out of the bowl. Stir in the Grand Marnier, then add the melted chocolate. Switch to a paddle attachment, then stir in the flour, baking powder and almonds. Wrap the dough in clingfilm, then refrigerate for 4 hours.

Preheat the oven to 160°C/320°F/Gas 3. Line a baking sheet with baking paper.

Roll the dough into about 20 walnut-sized balls. Put some caster sugar in one bowl and some icing sugar in another. Dip the cookie-dough balls in the caster sugar, then the icing sugar (*see also Basic Techniques, page 37*). Shake off any excess icing sugar and place on the prepared baking sheet, leaving a gap of 4–5cm (1½–2in) between them. Bake for 15–20 minutes.

Remove from the oven and transfer to a wire rack. Leave to cool for 15 minutes before serving.

Why not try ...
replacing the Grand Marnier with brandy, or you could use Baileys, which creates a really good flavour.

ANISE SEED BISCUITS

Growing up in Israel is a culinary delight. There are people from many different backgrounds, who bring all kinds of flavours and influences to food. One of these very special people was the mother of one of my childhood friends. She was originally from Morocco. Her kitchen was full of airtight containers filled with her homemade treats. My favourite was these anise seed biscuits, and I used many excuses to go to their house, just so I could eat some of these with mint tea.

Makes about 30 biscuits

180g (6¼oz) plain flour

1 tsp baking powder

60g (2oz) caster sugar

25ml (⅞fl oz) water

1 egg

25ml (⅞fl oz) vegetable oil

25g (⅞oz) anise seeds

Preheat the oven to 170°C/325°F/Gas 3. Grease a baking tray and line with baking paper.

Sift the flour and baking powder into a large bowl. In a separate bowl, mix together the sugar, water, egg, oil and anise seeds. Gradually add the wet ingredients to the flour and baking powder, then mix together using your hands, until you have a dough consistency.

Divide the dough in half, then roll out each piece on a floured surface, to a thickness of 3mm (⅛in). Using a fork, pierce the dough every 1cm (⅓in). Cut the dough into equal rectangles and place them on the baking tray. Bake for 18–20 minutes, or until light golden brown in colour.

MANDARIN PÂTE DE FRUITS

Makes 48 pieces

500g (1lb 2oz) mandarin purée
  (ready-made, available to
  purchase online)
12g (scant ½oz) pectin
550g (1lb 3oz) caster sugar, plus
  extra for coating
70g (2¼oz) glucose
3g (scant ⅛oz) citric acid

EQUIPMENT
325 x 265 x 50mm (12¾ x 10½ x 2in)
  baking tray
digital sugar thermometer

Put simply, this is a fruit jelly coated in sugar. We'd make 5kg (11lb) of these every two days, to be served to customers at the end of their meal. I found it amusing to learn how to make this typically French dessert, as it took me back to my childhood memory of eating jelly sweets! It takes some practice to make these perfectly, but, once you get the knack, it's worth the effort.

Grease the baking tray. Put the mandarin purée in a large, deep saucepan and bring to the boil.

Measure the pectin in a small container. In a bowl, put 50g (1¾oz) of the sugar and the pectin. Mix with your hands, making sure there are no lumps. In another bowl, add the remaining sugar and make a well in the middle. Pour in the glucose.

Add the sugar and pectin to the boiling purée and whisk gently. Bring it back to the boil, then add the sugar and glucose. Using the thermometer, measure the temperature of the mixture. When it is 108°C (226°F), add the citric acid and whisk to mix. Pour the mixture into the prepared tray and leave to set for at least 2 hours.

Carefully turn out the jelly onto a chopping board and cut into cubes using a hot, sharp knife. Roll the cubes in caster sugar, to coat.

Why not try ...
lemon, blood orange, passion fruit or lime. Any fruit purée that has the same consistency as the mandarin will work well for this recipe.

▶ *key stages illustrated overleaf*

MANDARIN PÂTE DE FRUITS KEY STAGES

1. Get everything ready before you start, with your ingredients measured into bowls, ready to use.

2. Add the sugar-and-pectin mixture to the boiling mandarin purée. Whisk gently.

3. Add the remaining sugar and the glucose.

4. Add the citric acid, and whisk to combine.

5. Pour the mixture into the prepared tray and leave to set.

VIOLET MACARONS

Makes about 20 macarons

WHITE CHOCOLATE GANACHE
150ml (5fl oz) whipping cream
150g (5oz) white chocolate

ALMOND PASTE
120g (4¼oz) icing sugar
120g (4¼oz) ground almonds
45g (1½oz) egg white
5 drops of violet flavouring

SYRUP
120g (4¼oz) caster sugar
40ml (1⅓fl oz) water
a pinch of purple food colouring
  powder

MERINGUE
45g (1½oz) egg whites
a pinch of salt
1½ tsp caster sugar

EQUIPMENT
digital thermometer
piping bag and round nozzle
silicone mat

Why not try ...
using a different flavour and colour to
suit your tastes – there are plenty to
choose from!

I was a keen and eager-to-impress pastry chef working in London when the restaurant manager asked me to make 800 macarons for a VIP event happening that week. 'Of course,' I replied. 'Not a problem.' But there was a problem: I had never made a macaron before! After panicking for a while, I pulled myself together and called a good friend of mine, who talked me through the process. I pulled off the macarons without a hitch and the team were suitably impressed, none the wiser that it was my first attempt!

The truth is, they aren't as daunting as you may think when staring in the window of a macaron shop in Paris. Follow the method to the letter, and, once you master the technique, you master the macaron.

First, make the white chocolate ganache. Put the cream in a saucepan and bring to the boil, then pour over the white chocolate. Using a hand blender, mix until you have a smooth ganache with no lumps. Refrigerate overnight.

NEXT DAY
Put all the paste ingredients in a bowl, mix to a paste and set aside.

Put all the ingredients for the syrup in a small saucepan and heat to 110°C (225°F), then start whisking the egg whites for the meringue. Once the syrup reaches 115°C (240°F), slowly pour it over the egg whites. Add the caster sugar to the meringue in three stages, while whisking. When the meringue temperature is 45°C (115°F), stop whisking and set aside.

Add a little of the meringue to the almond paste and stir to loosen the paste. Add the remaining meringue to the almond mixture in three stages, folding carefully; if you overwork the mixture, it won't hold its shape when you pipe it.

Preheat the oven to 140°C/275°F/Gas 1. Using a piping bag with a round nozzle, pipe the mixture onto a silicone mat, making the macarons to the desired size.

Bake for 10 minutes, turn the mat, then bake for another 5–10 minutes, depending on the size of the macarons. Line a separate baking tray with baking paper.

Leave to cool for 10 minutes, then transfer the macaron shells to the lined baking tray to cool completely. Spoon some ganache into the centre of a macaron shell, then sandwich with another. Repeat with the remaining shells and ganache.

MA'AMOUL

The ma'amoul is a beautiful Arabian delight. It's a small shortbread pastry filled with pistachios, other nuts or dried fruit such as dates or prunes. It's very popular in the Middle East, especially in Israel, where you can find it pretty much everywhere. Traditionally, it provides the finish to a Ramadan feast and is enjoyed during any big holiday, and even during Easter for the Christian Arab communities.

Makes about 30 ma'amoul

FILLING
250g (9oz) dried prunes
75g (2½oz) ground almonds
1 tbsp mixed spice

DOUGH
250g (9oz) plain flour
75g (2½oz) semolina
2½ tsp baking powder
40g (1½oz) caster sugar
seeds of ½ vanilla pod
60ml (2fl oz) vegetable oil
60ml (2fl oz) water
100g (3½oz) butter
a few drops of rose water

icing sugar (for dusting)

Line a baking tray with baking paper.

Before making the filling, soak the prunes in boiling water for 10 minutes, then drain. Place all the ingredients for the filling in a blender and whizz to a purée consistency. If it seems too thick, add a little hot water. Put the mixture in the fridge for at least 30 minutes, to set.

Meanwhile, put all the dough ingredients in an electric mixer. Using the paddle attachment, combine until you have a smooth dough. Divide into 25g (⅞oz) pieces and, using a rolling pin, roll out to form discs 3–5mm (⅛in–⅕in) thick.

Preheat the oven to 180°C/350°F/Gas 4. Remove the filling from the fridge and, using wet hands, roll into olive-sized balls. Place one in the middle of each disc and bring the dough up around the sides and seal, so the filling is covered. Roll into smooth balls and make grooves in the surface using a fork.

Place the ma'amoul on the prepared baking tray and bake for about 15 minutes, or until very light golden on top. To serve, dust with icing sugar.

> **Why not try ...**
> replacing the prunes with dates – use the date baklava filling (*see page 149*).

OATMEAL COOKIES

Makes 24 cookies

200g (7oz) butter, room temperature

200g (7oz) light brown sugar

2 eggs, room temperature

150g (5oz) plain flour

½ tsp cinnamon

½ tsp baking powder

210g (7½oz) jumbo oats

60g (2oz) pecan nuts, chopped

60g (2oz) raisins

I came across this recipe on my honeymoon in the Caribbean. The food was healthy, tasty and freshly made each day. After my yoga session first thing every morning, I'd start breakfast with a freshly baked oatmeal cookie. I've been making them for my family and friends ever since.

Beat the butter and sugar in a large bowl, adding the eggs one by one. Sieve the flour, cinnamon and baking powder into the mixture and combine all the ingredients, then add the oats, pecan nuts and raisins.

Place the cookie dough on a floured surface and divide into two halves. Roll each piece into a sausage shape, wrap in clingfilm and place in the freezer for at least 2 hours.

Preheat the oven to 170°C/325°F/Gas 3. Line a baking sheet with baking paper. Remove the cookie dough from the freezer and cut off the clingfilm. Place each cookie-dough sausage on a chopping board and cut into 1cm (⅓in) slices using a sharp knife (*see Basic Techniques, pages 34–5*). Arrange them on the lined baking sheet, leaving a gap of 5cm (2in) in between them. Bake for 12–15 minutes, until the cookies look set.

Transfer to a wire rack and leave to cool for 15 minutes before serving.

Why not try ...
adding your favourite dried fruit or chocolate chips.

MINI CINNAMON DOUGHNUTS

Makes about 30 mini doughnuts

225g (8oz) strong white flour

25g (⅞oz) caster sugar, plus extra
  for coating

½ tsp salt

110ml (3¾fl oz) water

15g (½oz) yeast

1 egg

15g (½oz) butter, softened

vegetable oil (for spraying or brushing
  and deep-frying)

½ tsp ground cinnamon (for coating)

EQUIPMENT

sugar thermometer

Working in restaurants, whenever I made standard-sized doughnuts I'd often have dough left over. I'd roll the dough into a long sausage shape and cut it into small pieces using a dough scraper, then deep-fry them for a minute and roll them in cinnamon sugar. At the end of service, I'd put them out on the pass for the kitchen staff, and they'd be gone in 3 seconds!

To make the dough, put the flour, sugar, salt, water, yeast and egg in an electric mixer fitted with a dough hook. Knead for 7–10 minutes, then add the butter and continue to knead until well incorporated. Alternatively, knead by hand (*see Basic Techniques, page 28*). Put the dough in the fridge for 2–3 hours, until it has doubled in size.

Cut a sheet of baking paper into strips 5cm (2in) wide. Spray or brush a baking tray with oil and line with the strips of baking paper. Spray or brush the strips with oil.

Place the dough on a lightly floured surface, divide into four pieces and roll them into sausages of the same size and shape. Using a dough cutter, slice each dough sausage into 2cm (¾in) pieces. Place them on the baking paper, leaving a gap in between them. Spray or brush the tops of the doughnuts with oil and cover with clingfilm. Leave to prove for 15–20 minutes.

Heat some vegetable oil in a large, deep saucepan (the pan should be three-quarters full), using a sugar thermometer to ensure that the temperature doesn't exceed 180°C (350°F). Deep-fry the doughnuts in three batches, for 4–5 minutes per batch. Ensure that the oil temperature is maintained at 160–170°C (320–325°F), and keep turning and moving the doughnuts in the oil. Once they are golden brown, place them on kitchen paper to allow the excess oil to drain off.

Half-fill a large bowl with caster sugar and mix in the cinnamon. Roll the doughnuts in the cinnamon sugar to finish.

Why not try ...
rolling the doughnuts in a vanilla sugar,
as an alternative to cinnamon.

▶ key stages illustrated overleaf

MINI CINNAMON DOUGHNUTS KEY STAGES

1. Line a greased baking tray with strips of baking paper, then spray or brush with oil.

2. Roll the dough into four equal-sized sausages.

3. Cut each sausage into slices using a dough cutter.

4. Place the slices on the baking-paper strips, leaving space around each one.

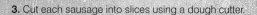

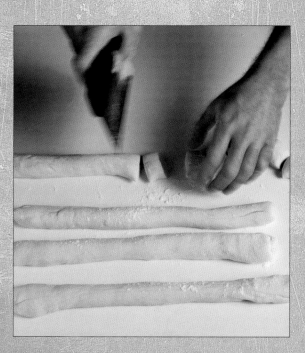

5. Place the deep-fried doughnuts on kitchen paper.

6. Roll the doughnuts in cinnamon sugar, to coat.

169

Millionaire Shortbread

Making millionaire shortbread can be a daunting prospect, because you have to get three separate layers to work perfectly together. However, it's actually quite easy to make if you follow the recipe, and the results are well worth the effort.

Preheat the oven to 170°C/325°F/Gas 3. Put all the shortbread ingredients in a large bowl and mix together using both hands. The mixture should first resemble fine breadcrumbs, then stick together to form a dough.

Roll out the dough on a floured surface, to a thickness of 6–8mm (¼–⅓in); try to roll it to the size and shape of your baking tray. Make sure the dough is an even depth throughout. Transfer the dough to the tray, using the rolling pin to help support it. Pierce holes all over the dough, using a fork. Bake the dough for about 20 minutes, or until golden brown on top. Leave to cool.

Once the shortbread is cool, you can start to prepare the caramel. Place all the ingredients in a large, deep saucepan, bring to the boil and simmer for 8 minutes, or until the caramel is a light golden colour. Pour over the shortbread and, using a palette knife, spread the caramel evenly and leave to cool for at least 20 minutes.

Put the dark chocolate in a bowl over a pan of boiling water and melt gently. Pour over the cooled caramel and, again using a palette knife, spread evenly over the top. Try not to overwork the chocolate, as it will start to set. Sprinkle Maldon sea salt over the chocolate.

Once the chocolate has cooled and set, turn out the millionaire shortbread onto a chopping board and cut into pieces using a hot knife.

Makes 15 pieces

SHORTBREAD
250g (9oz) butter
160g (5½oz) icing sugar
50g (1¾oz) ground almonds
2 eggs
seeds of ½ vanilla pod
420g (14¾oz) plain flour

CARAMEL
180g (6¼oz) butter
60g (2oz) golden syrup
360g (12½oz) condensed milk
2 tsp sea salt

TOPPING
225g (8oz) dark chocolate, broken
   into pieces
Maldon sea salt (for sprinkling)

EQUIPMENT
325 x 265 x 50mm (12¾ x 10½ x 2in)
   baking tray
palette knife

MINIATURE MIXED-NUT COOKIES

Makes 40 cookies

200g (7oz) almonds

200g (7oz) pistachios

200g (7oz) pecan nuts

200g (7oz) caster sugar, plus
   extra for dipping

1 tsp mixed spice

2 eggs

1 egg yolk

icing sugar, for dipping

When I worked in London, I used to fill big glass jars with miniature delights for guests to enjoy with their coffee. This was one of the favourites. They are not only delicious, but with the pistachio green colour they also look fantastic.

Line a baking sheet with baking paper. Put all the nuts and the sugar in a food processor and whizz until all the nuts are ground. Transfer to a large bowl and combine with the mixed spice and eggs. Roll into walnut-sized balls.

Preheat the oven to 160°C/320°F/Gas 3. Put some caster sugar in one bowl and some icing sugar in another. Dip the cookie-dough balls into the caster sugar, then the icing sugar (*see Basic Techniques, page 37*). Shake off any excess icing sugar and place on the prepared baking sheet, leaving 4–5cm (1½–2in) between them.

Bake for 15–20 minutes, until the cookies are slightly golden on the bottom and cracked on the top. Leave to cool on a wire rack for 15 minutes before serving.

Why not try ...
brazil or macadamia nuts – there's no need to stick to my choices.

BASIC RECIPES

SOURDOUGH STARTER

Put the yeast and water in a large container. When the yeast has dissolved, add the sugar. Stir in the flour with a wooden spoon.

If your starter is in a bowl, cover the bowl with clingfilm; alternatively, store it in a Kilner (preserving) jar. Leave the starter in a warm place for 3 days, stirring once a day. It should bubble and have a strong sour smell.

AFTER THREE DAYS
Refresh the starter with the flour and warm water. Stir to combine and leave in a warm place for 24 hours.

Move the starter to the fridge, refreshing after each use or once every 10 days.

DAY ONE
8g (¼oz) fresh yeast or 1 tsp fast-action dried yeast
145ml (5fl oz) warm water
1 tsp caster sugar
135g (4¾oz) strong white flour

DAY FOUR
170g (6oz) strong white flour
180ml (6fl oz) warm water

PAINSWICK STARTER

DAY ONE
Put all the ingredients in a bowl and whisk for about 5 minutes. Cover with clingfilm and leave in a warm place overnight.

DAY TWO
Add the rye flour to the mixture and whisk for 5 minutes. Cover again and leave in a warm place for about 24 hours.

DAY THREE
Check if the mixture is active – bubbles should be forming on the top of the dough and it should have increased substantially in volume.

Pour the mixture through a colander, into a bowl. Discard the contents of the colander, including the sultanas.

Move the starter to the fridge, refreshing with equal amounts of warm water and flour (half rye flour and half strong white flour) after each use or once every 10 days.

To make a rye starter, follow this recipe, but use boiling water rather than Earl Grey tea.

Painswick Loaf (page 62)

DAY ONE
125g (4½oz) strong white flour
125g (4½oz) dark rye flour
150ml (5fl oz) Earl Grey tea (put 2 teabags in 150ml/5fl oz boiling water and leave for 20 minutes)
150g (5oz) yogurt
50g (1¾oz) sultanas

DAY TWO
1 tbsp rye flour

WILD GARLIC PESTO

Wild Garlic Tear-and-Share (page 65)

Place all the ingredients in a food processor and whizz for 5–7 minutes, until you have a smooth paste. If it's too thick, add a few more drops of olive oil.

Store the pesto in an airtight jar. It will keep for up to 1 month.

500g (1lb 2oz) wild garlic leaves
100ml (3½fl oz) extra virgin olive oil
60g (2oz) Parmesan cheese, grated
40g (1½oz) peanuts

RICH TOMATO SAUCE

Sourdough Pizza (page 104)

Preheat the oven to 180°C/350°F/Gas 4.

Put the tomatoes in the ovenproof dish, together with the olive oil, garlic and seasoning. Stir well, then cover with the lid and put the dish in the oven for 3 hours.

While still hot, transfer the tomato sauce to a food processor and whizz for 5 minutes. Allow it to cool completely before storing.

Stored in an airtight container or jar, this sauce will keep for up to 2 weeks in the fridge, or 3 months in the freezer.

15 tomatoes, cubed
2 tbsp olive oil
2 garlic cloves, crushed and finely
  chopped
salt and freshly ground black pepper

EQUIPMENT
large ovenproof dish with a lid

Cauliflower Moneybags (page 87)

1 x 300g (11oz) jar of tahini
juice of 3 lemons
1 clove of garlic, crushed and finely
  chopped
1 tomato, quartered and deseeded
salt, for seasoning

TAHINI SAUCE

Pour the tahini into a large bowl, scraping the jar with a spoon. Fill the jar with lukewarm water and add it to the bowl. Whisk until smooth, making sure there are no lumps. Add the lemon juice and garlic.

Using a sharp knife, cut the skin off the tomato quarters, then finely chop them into cubes. Add the tomato to the tahini and, using your whisk, stir until well combined. Add salt to taste.

The tahini sauce will keep in the fridge for 3–4 days.

200g (7oz) pistachios (peeled,
  to give them their green colour)
60ml (2fl oz) vegetable oil

PISTACHIO PASTE

Preheat the oven to 180°C/350°F/Gas 4. Line a baking tray with aluminium foil.

Spread out the pistachios on the prepared baking tray and roast for 8–10 minutes.

While still hot, transfer the nuts to a food processor and whizz, adding 2 tablespoons of oil every 3 minutes, until the paste is smooth and thick. You want it to be pourable.

CRÈME PATISSIÈRE

Line a deep baking tray with clingfilm.

Pour the milk into a medium-sized saucepan. Scrape the seeds from the vanilla pod and add them to the milk, along with the pod. Heat the milk and bring to the boil.

Put the sugar, flour and egg yolks in a small mixing bowl, then whisk until you have a paste consistency.

Once the milk has reached boiling point, add one third to the paste and whisk to loosen. Pour the mixture back into the saucepan and reduce the heat. Continue to whisk until the mixture thickens. This will take 2–3 minutes.

Pass the mixture through a fine sieve, into the prepared tray. Place another layer of clingfilm over the top and smooth out the surface of the crème patissière. Leave to cool at room temperature, then store in the fridge until needed. It will keep for up to 3 days.

Nutella Brioche (variation; page 116)

250ml (9fl oz) milk
¼ vanilla pod
50g (1¾oz) caster sugar
20g (⅔oz) plain flour
60g (2oz) egg yolk (about 3 egg yolks)

CRYSTALLIZED ROSE PETALS

Preheat the oven to 90°C/200°F, or the lowest setting you have. Line a baking sheet with baking paper.

Put some sugar in one bowl and some egg white in another. Dip each rose petal in the egg white, shake off the excess, then dip in the sugar. Spread out the petals on the baking sheet.

Put the rose petals in the oven and bake for about 3 hours. To test whether they're ready, try breaking one; if it's still soft, bake them for a bit longer. They should be completely crispy.

Store the crystallized rose petals in an airtight container, at room temperature. They will keep for up to 1 month.

Pistachio & Rose Cakes (page 131)

caster sugar
egg white
rose petals

CROISSANT DOUGH

DOUGH
400g (14oz) strong white flour
60ml (2fl oz) cold water
14g (½oz) fresh yeast or 7g (¼oz)
  fast-action dried yeast
60g (2oz) butter
40g (1½oz) caster sugar

BUTTER
340g (12oz) butter
110g (scant 4oz) caster sugar
30g (1oz) strong white flour

Place all the dough ingredients in a large bowl, bring together and knead for 10 minutes. Cover the bowl and leave to prove for 2 hours, or until the dough has doubled in size.

Meanwhile, prepare the butter. Put all the ingredients in an electric mixer with a paddle attachment and beat for 5 minutes, or until the mixture is very soft and spreadable.

On a floured work surface, roll out the dough into a rectangular shape (1). Spread half of the butter mixture over two-thirds of the dough, leaving a 2cm (¾in) border (2).

Now you're going to fold the dough into thirds. Fold the non-buttered third onto the middle third of the dough (3), then again onto the last third. Leave the dough to rest on the worktop for 5 minutes, then gently roll it out to form a rectangle again (4 & 5). Fold the dough as before, this time with no butter mixture (6). Wrap the dough in clingfilm and refrigerate for 1 hour.

Put the second half of the butter in the electric mixer and whizz to soften. Remove the dough from the fridge and roll it into a rectangle once again, folding as before, with the remaining butter. Put the dough in the fridge for another hour, before use.

The dough can be kept in the fridge for up to 3 days, or in the freezer for 3 months.

Parmesan & Poppy-seed Puff Twists (page 99)

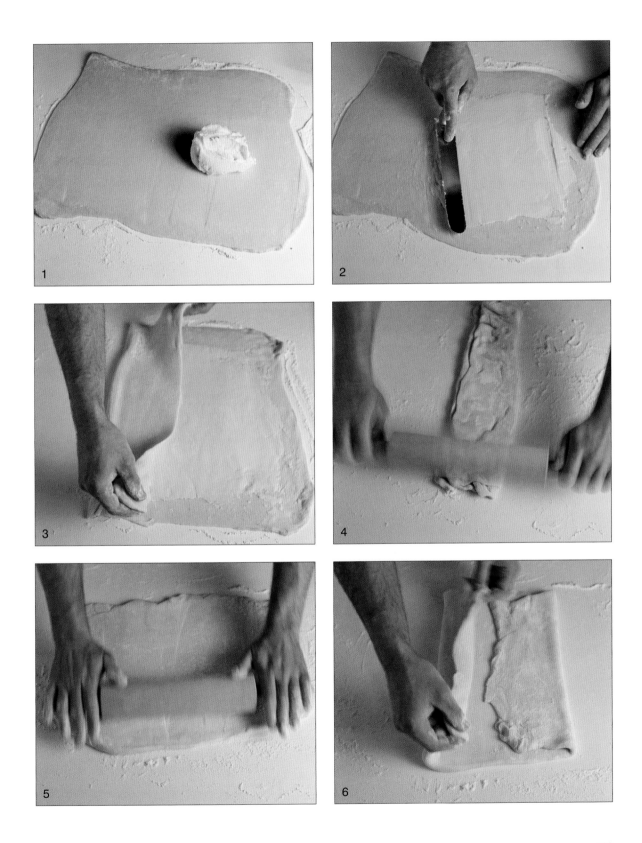

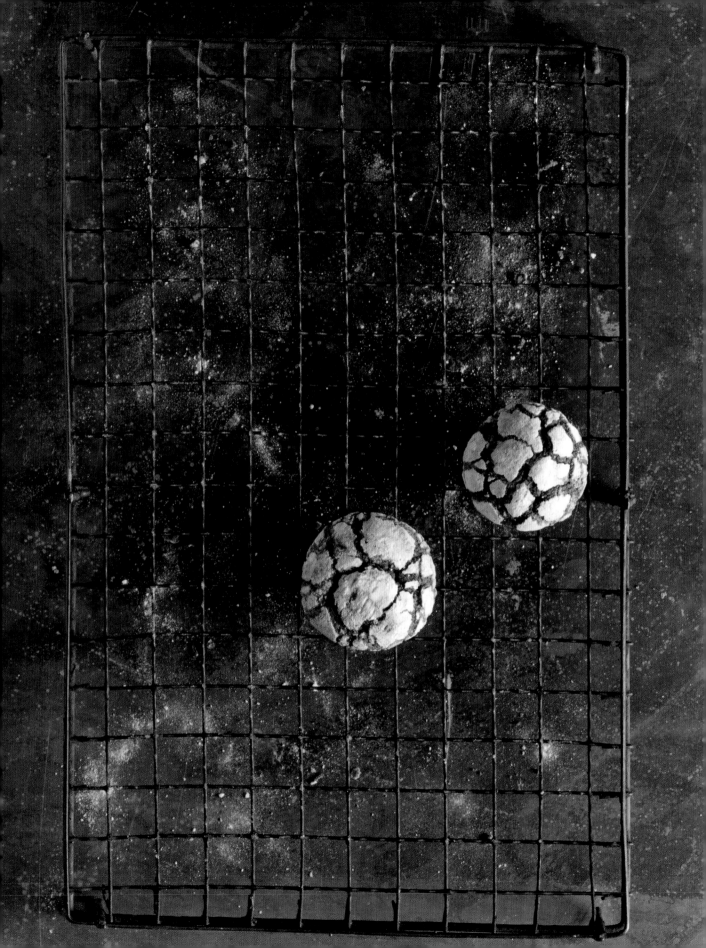

INDEX

CONVERSION NOTES

OVEN TEMPERATURE

Centigrade temperatures given in the recipes are for conventional ovens. For fan-assisted ovens, reduce the temperature by 20°C.

CUP MEASUREMENTS

Metric and imperial quantities are included for all recipes. For standard cup conversions, use the guidelines below:

¼ cup = 60ml	2fl oz
⅓ cup = 80ml	3fl oz
½ cup = 125ml	4fl oz
1 cup = 250ml	9fl oz

ACKNOWLEDGEMENTS

I would like to thank my publisher Nick Eddison, editor Tessa Monina and designer Braz Atkins, who I've worked very closely with for the past six months. Thank you for believing in what the book represents and its recipes, and seeing that we have something new and different in this busy world of baking!

A big thanks to Katie Golsby, who has worked so hard on editing and checking every recipe in the book to the letter!

I would also like to thank Sue Atkinson, who shot such beautiful pictures, and her assistant Anna.

Thanks to Matthew Fort for writing the foreword, and for his ongoing support.

A huge thanks to my wife Yvonne and son George for their support and patience over the last few incredibly crazy years. They have been with me every step of the way, through the highs and the lows.

And, finally, I couldn't have done it without the help of our family: Bridget, Margaret, Tony, Ged and my parents Soni and Efi, who have been so supportive and generous, from helping in farmers markets to dishwashing and helping with child care, and who provided an open ear whenever I needed one.

EDDISON·SADD EDITIONS

Creative Director Nick Eddison
Managing Editor Tessa Monina
Project Editor Katie Golsby
Proofreader Nikky Twyman
Indexer Cathy Heath
Designer Brazzle Atkins
Production Sarah Rooney

Eddison Sadd would like to thank Lara Jane Thorpe for the photographs used in step 4 on page 119, and Abi at the wonderful Vintage Mary of Stroud.

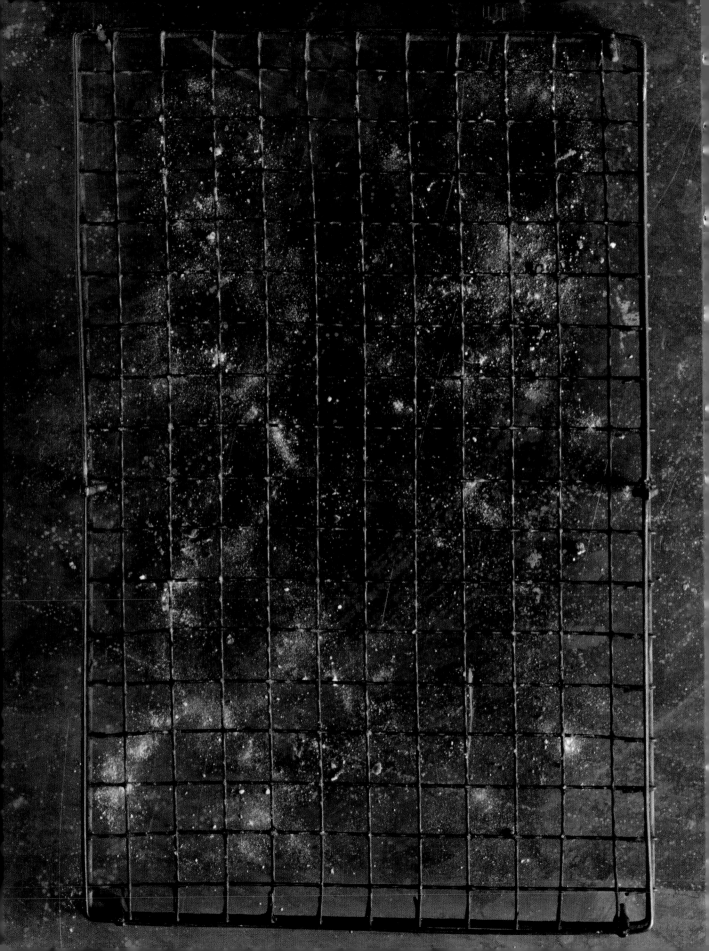